Contents

How to Get an A Grade

Effective learning involves reducing difficult topics into smaller, "bite-sized" chunks.

Every revision guide, card or coursebook from PushMe Press comes with its own website consisting of summaries, handouts, games, model essays, revision notes and more. Each website community is supported by the best teachers in the country.

At the end of each chapter you will see an i-pu-sh web link that you can type into your web browser along with a QR code that can be scanned by our free app.

These links will give you immediate access to the additional resources you need to "Get an A Grade" by providing you with the relevant information needed.

Getting an A Grade has never been easier.

Download our FREE How to Get an A Grade in Philosophy App for your phone or tablet and get up-to-date information that accompanies this book and the whole PushMe Press range.

http://philosophy.pushmepress.com/download

Philosophy of Religion

A2 Revision Guide for OCR

Brian Poxon

Published by Inducit Learning Ltd trading as PushMe Press

Mid Somerset House, Southover, Wells

Somerset BA5 1UH, United Kingdom

www.pushmepress.com

First published in 2013, second edition 2014

ISBN: 978-1-910038-73-4

Religious Language

KEY TERMS

- **ANALOGY** - When two things are compared as similar because they share common features, eg the brain is like a computer.

- **ANALYTIC STATEMENT** - The internal logic of the sentence gives it its meaning.

- **BLIK** - A way of looking at the world. (**HARE**)

- **COGNITIVE** - Language that carries meaning, and puts forward a proposition, provable true or false.

- **EQUIVOCAL** - Where the same word is used in two different and unrelated ways, eg someone is at the sink, and someone is starting to sink.

- **FALSIFICATION PRINCIPLE** - A statement is putting forward a genuine scientific proposition if there are conditions under which that proposition can be falsified.

- **LANGUAGE GAME** - Individual terms have meaning because of the way they are used within a group. (Wittgenstein) A form of life is the activities that the group performs using this language.

- **MYTH** - A story which conveys a religious belief or truth.

- **NON-COGNITIVE** - Does not carry meaning in a factual manner, and is not putting forward a proposition provable true or false.

- **REALIST** - Claims that refer to something that objectively exists, not something that exists just within the community of believers (anti-realist).

- **STRONG VERIFICATION PRINCIPLE** - A statement carries meaning only if it is either analytic or empirically verifiable.

- **UNIVOCAL** - Where the same word is used in two different contexts but means the same thing: a black cat and a cat on the mat. The word cat has the one meaning in both sentences.

- **VIA NEGATIVA** (the Apophatic Way) - The way of talking about God by saying what He is not.

- **VIA POSITIVA** (the Cataphatic Way) - The way of talking about God by saying what He is.

- **WEAK VERIFICATION PRINCIPLE** - A statement carries meaning only if it is "either analytic or can be shown by experience to be probably true". (**BURNS** and **LAW**)

THE VIA NEGATIVA (VN)

The **VN** is also known as **THE APOPHATIC WAY**, taken from the Greek verb apophēmi, which means "to deny". The VN is an attempt to speak of God using **NEGATION** and stems from the mystical religious tradition, which emphasises the quest to find unity with God. However, God lies **BEYOND** ordinary perception and cannot be described in the same way in which we describe other objects: for example, this teapot is green or that sweatshirt is large. God cannot be described adequately using "the positive", because He is **INEFFABLE**; He defies expression or description.

When we attempt to use the affirmative and use words such as "powerful" about a strong person, we mean something completely different when we say God is powerful. This is called **EQUIVOCAL LANGUAGE**.

We can get some knowledge of God, by the way of the negative - by saying what **GOD IS NOT** - and joining such "not" statements together to arrive at a closer idea of **WHAT GOD IS**. In this sense, language for the person who advocates the **VN** is not descriptive or containing knowledge, (**COGNITIVE**), but, as Cole notes, being used in a "functional and evocative" way.

For example, I could get directions to Fraser Street by a series of negatives (don't turn right at the junction). **MAIMONIDES** (12th C), used the example of a ship; by about the time of the 10th negative answer to questions concerning what a ship is, the enquirer had almost arrived at an accurate idea of a ship.

The illustration of the man asking directions works when there are only three or four options. He knew where Fraser Street was because we discounted every other option for him. But can we use this way for a description of God? No, but with a series of questions, and by joining the answers together, we should get closer to what God is via the negative.

The **VN** has a long history. You may recognise some Platonic tones, where there is an ultimate good beyond the cave world we inhabit, and of which we only see shadows. In the 3rd C **PLOTINUS**, a neo-Platonist (a movement which built on the work of Plato but also altered/adapted Platonism), argued that it was impossible to know the good as it is entirely separate from the world.

ST AUGUSTINE (4th C) and **DIONYSIUS** (also known as **PSEUDO-DIONYSIUS**, 6th C), both wrote about the use of the VN as part of the mystical tradition. Dionysius noted three stages, or "states of knowledge" (**JORDAN**) when talking about God.

1. VIA NEGATIVA

States what God is not, because God is beyond all human categories of knowledge and being. He is "not" anything which we would try to describe such as "life" or "oneness" or "good". "There is no speaking of it, nor name, nor knowledge of it. Darkness and light, error and truth ... [God] is none of these." (**HICK**) So God is beyond any positive assertion.

2. STATE OF AFFIRMATION

Affirm what we know God is: we do know God has been revealed in the Bible as good and just. But these terms can only be taken symbolically.

3. QUALIFICATION

When we say God is loving, He is utterly beyond loving as affirmed in the mystical tradition, which is always looking "beyond" descriptions which are limited by human language. Maimonides also argues that the **INEFFABILITY** of God cannot be expressed by positive assertions about God.

Strengths

1. The **VN** avoids **ANTHROPOMORPHISM** (describing God in human terms) - It can stop people getting the wrong idea about God as being "warrior like", and taking this literally as saying that God is some kind of Divine Warrior. The **VN** argues that God is entirely "not" like us.

2. **LIMITATIONS OF LANGUAGE** - As a vessel to adequately describe God. Reason, logic and arguments are blunt tools when it comes to the spiritual mystery that is God. **AHLUWALIA** points out that anything other than the idea that God is mystery makes God too small.

3. **INEFFABILITY** - The **VN** goes beyond our everyday experience, and allows for recognition that God is not "over there" or, indeed, located anywhere, or "like this". God is entirely ineffable.

Weaknesses

1. **CONTRADICTION** - Between God's ineffability and the revelation of the Bible of the physical person Jesus Christ. Dionysius may in fact have accepted Christ as "God revealed", ie, a manifestation of God, but this is not "God hidden", who remains ineffable.

2. **REALIST** - Affirmations made by believers seem to go further. God has certain positive characteristics, for example, a warrior or a mighty king. Within many of the world's religions, **TRUTH CLAIMS ARE NOT NEGATIVELY EXPRESSED**. Judaism, Christianity and Islam believe that God has in fact revealed his nature and affirms that nature in their respective scriptures. Christian theologians argue that at the heart of the Christian faith is the affirmation that God is involved in the world, rather than beyond matter, life, humanity and any description.

3. **DAVIES** - Does not think negatives can get us closer to the actual thing we are trying to describe.

4. **BEGS THE QUESTION** - Every time we give a negative answer, we are showing that we already know what God is, and so the VN only works for those who already know who and what God is, which seems self-contradictory.

5. **DEATH BY A THOUSAND QUALIFICATIONS** - By continually saying God is not this, and God is not that, **FLEW** contends that there is little difference between saying that "God is anything we can affirm" and "God does not exist" - by saying that God is invisible, soundless, incorporeal and so on, there is very little difference between our definition of God and our definition of nothingness; we argue God out of existence by "a thousand qualifications". (**AHLUWALIA**)

Key quotes

1. *"We do not know what God is. God Himself does not know what He is because He is not anything. Literally God is not, because He transcends being." John Scot Erigena (9th C)*

2. *"God is utterly transcendent, totally ineffable, indescribable and incapable of being conceptualised by the human mind." Hick on Dionysius*

3. *"Perhaps a more balanced approach [than complete reliance on the VN] would be to argue that we need both the via negativa and the via positiva." Wilkinson and Campbell*

4. *"The negative way is the way of darkness, suffering, silence, letting go, and even nothingness." Sheldrake and Fox*

Confusions to avoid

People who take the VN approach do think it is possible to talk about God, but God is beyond what we say in human language. To say God is loving does not have any frame of reference as we only know what loving is in human understanding. God is "beyond assertion". (**DIONYSIUS**) But anything we say about God, even the negative, does not tell us about God, so also "beyond denial" as language is **EQUIVOCAL**. So the experience of God is real, and is what the mystics seek by union with Him, and although the "infinite can penetrate the finite" there can be "no corresponding language statements made" and hence God is ineffable.

THE USE OF ANALOGY

AQUINAS was very familiar with the work of both Dionysius and Maimonides. Aquinas rejected the via negativa because he thought that it is possible to speak positively of God in non-literal and analogical terms. Hence he rejected **EQUIVOCAL LANGUAGE** as it has no link between what we say using our language to describe things available to us (ie something is beautiful or good) and how we use the same language when referring to God.

Does this mean that when we talk about beautiful and good in our language, this means exactly the same when applied to God? This sort of use of language is known as **UNIVOCAL** and Aquinas went on to reject this also, as things do not mean exactly the same when they are used in description of a thing in this world and when used to describe God. "God is strong" and "I am strong" do not mean the same thing.

Aquinas' alternative was to make use of **ANALOGICAL LANGUAGE**. which carries some kind of shared understanding between what it means when describing an object and when that same term is used to describe God. There is some **COMPARISON** that can be made between two different things when using analogy. **WE CAN SAY SOMETHING**. For example, to say a computer is like a brain is to note similarities between those two things, like they both have a kind of electrical circuit, they both receive input and produce output and they both process data, without saying they are the same.

Aquinas goes on to define two types of analogy that can be used. The first is the **ANALOGY OF ATTRIBUTION**. This is when there is a **CAUSAL RELATIONSHIP** that can be described by the terms being used. For example, if someone says that the piece of furniture is good, we can say that the carpenter must be good. Now, we do not mean that the carpenter has a polished finish and finely shaped handles (that would be univocal language); neither do we say that there is no connection between how we are using good to describe the piece of furniture and good to describe the carpenter (that would be equivocal language). We see that there is some causal link between saying that the furniture is good, and that the carpenter is good. **BECAUSE** the carpenter is good, the furniture is good. The example that Aquinas gave is that of a bull's urine. If one sees a sample of the bull's urine and it is healthy (not cloudy etc), then we can **ATTRIBUTE THIS TO THE HEALTH OF THE BULL**. There is a causal link between the two.

Aquinas argued that this meant we can, by the analogy of attribution, begin to **AFFIRM SOME THINGS OF GOD**. As God is the creator of the world, **WE CAN ATTRIBUTE THE GOODNESS OF THE WORLD TO THE GOODNESS OF GOD** in the same way we can say that the good quality of the urine is due to the good quality of the bull.

Aquinas' second use of analogy is the **ANALOGY OF PROPORTION**. This simply means when we use a word like "good", and we say God is good, what we are saying is that **THERE IS A WAY TO BE GOOD THAT BELONGS TO GOD**, just like there is a way for a person to be good that is appropriate for a person. There is an understanding between the use of the words, but there is also a difference, as **EACH IS USED PROPORTIONATELY TO THE SUBJECT**. So, when we say humans are powerful and God is powerful, we are saying that God is powerful in a greater way than humans could ever be.

We are saying that good is what it means for something to act well according to its **NATURE** - for a computer to be good is very different from what it means for an umbrella to be good, but both have their way of being good. This is the way in which Aquinas is using these terms (such as good or powerful), and it has links back to Aristotle's function argument.

SO BY ANALOGY THERE ARE FORMS OF LANGUAGE THAT CAN PROVIDE SOME WAYS OF TALKING ABOUT GOD THAT CARRY MEANING AND UNDERSTANDING

There is something in common in the terms being used - which is more than there is in equivocal use of language, and affirmative in a way that the via negativa could never be.

RAMSEY also made use of analogy to argue that it is possible to speak meaningfully about God. Ramsey noted that we can use **MODELS** when talking about God. If we say that God is loving, we have a model of loving because we know what loving is in human terms; the example of it we see in human interactions acts as some kind of model and gives us understanding of what loving means.

However, because we are talking about **GOD'S LOVE**, we have to **QUALIFY** our model. The models are useful, but they do not paint the whole picture - they are limited. Whilst humans model love, God is **INFINITELY LOVING**; without this qualification, we are just left with our model of what human love looks like.

This model and qualifier idea can lead to an insight into the quality being spoken about, in this case, the love of God, and Ramsey called such insight a **DISCLOSURE**. At this point, the qualified model has helped take us "beyond" to some disclosure about God. He used this argument to criticise the narrowness of the **VERIFICATION PRINCIPLE**, which, with its focus on empirical facts, did not take account of the empirical meaning found through personal "disclosure experiences".

Strengths

1. Analogy avoids **ANTHROPOMORPHISM**, where God is given human qualities, because both Aquinas' analogy of proportion and Ramsey's models and qualifiers, avoid saying that "this describes God". They both qualify their use of language when applying things found in human experience to God.

2. **POSITIVE** - Analogy enables a person to say something positive of God which might be more appropriate to the experience of most believers than that of the **VN**. At the same time, both Aquinas and Ramsey acknowledge the limited nature of language when used to try to describe God.

3. **COMPLEXITY** - By taking human experience as a starting reference point, Aquinas and Ramsey think that analogy can give insight into complex ideas such as God as all-loving and all-powerful.

Weaknesses

1. **ATTRIBUTING EVIL** - Should we not also attribute the evil of the world to God? This would then weaken Aquinas' idea of what type of God he is wishing to put forward by the use of analogy. **HUME** argues that we tend to use whatever analogy supports our existing belief. In looking at the world as it is, what qualities would we attribute to its maker? **DAWKINS** argues it is the world that would indicate a fight for survival rather than a world which can be attributed to a loving God.

2. **ASSUMES SOMETHING** - To use the analogy of attribution

assumes we know something of the nature of God in order for us to say that "a good world" is indicative of "a good God", so this may be confirming what a person already believes. Analogy also "assumes some similarity between the humans and God" (**EYRE**); the opposite conclusion might be equally valid, that God and humans share no similarities.

3. **SWINBURNE** has argued that we do not need to use analogy at all, as univocal language is sufficient when talking of God. When we call humans good and God good, we are using the word univocally, which is sufficient, carries meaning and can be understood.

4. **BARTH** has criticised analogy because knowledge of God cannot be gained from creation. Knowledge of God by its very nature, argues Barth, is only given by revelation from God.

Key quotes

1. *"It seems that no word can be used literally of God." Aquinas in Summa Theologiae*
2. *"Analogy enables language drawn from the spatio-temporal universe to be applied to a timeless and spaceless God and for this language to be held to be true, but the content of this language is extremely limited." Vardy*
3. *"The most we can say is that: Under the analogy of attribution, God has whatever it takes to create goodness (for instance) in human beings - but we don't know what it is. Under the analogy of proportion, it is true that God is good in whatever way it is appropriate for God to be good. We do not, however, know in what way it is appropriate for God to be good." Vardy*
4. *"Religious language consists of 'disclosure models' that are made up of both analogy and existential depth." Jackson on Ramsey*

Confusions to avoid

Both Aquinas and Ramsey are very clear that the use of analogy is still limited by human language. It would be wrong to say that they think they have found a way in which God can be adequately described. If you said that the way Usain Bolt runs is similar to the way in which an arrow leaves the bow and reaches its target, you are not saying that Bolt is a thin aluminium alloy shaft attached to an arrowhead fired from a 60 pound bow. What you are saying is that the speed with which he is released from the blocks has similarities to the way in which the arrow is fired from the bow, as is the way in which he runs straight and true, and with speed, towards a final target. The archery analogy "points towards"; it helps provide a comparison which highlights similar features between one thing and another.

THE USE OF MYTH

A **MYTH** is a story which conveys a religious belief or truth, or which points to a deeper reality, but is not factually true. A myth can include the use of symbols or metaphors or other literary devices, which are used to convey important truth(s) or unfold a worldview. Myths often deal with issues of ultimate significance such as the creation of the world, human identity, suffering, evil, morality and purpose.

Many Christians think that the **CREATION STORIES** are not meant to be read in a factual manner, but as myth, and are attempts by the writer(s) to point the reader towards things like structure within the universe, rhythm and order within creation, a creator who desires a relationship with humanity and the idea of work being part of the purpose of mankind. To ask whether a myth is "true" in a historical or scientific sense is the wrong question, just as one would not ask if poetry is "true".

As creation stories convey "truths" about the worldview of that community, it could be argued that there is **COGNITIVE MEANING** contained within them and this will be important when we come to study the **VERIFICATION PRINCIPLE** and how that principle seeks to measure how meaning is carried in language.

In the 20th C. **BULTMANN** argued that the New Testament must be **DEMYTHOLOGISED** if truth is to be discovered in it. Scientific understanding will not allow us to read scripture, and accounts such as a literal virgin birth, as previous generations did, which was in a very simplistic, "supernatural" and non-scientific way. The writers of the Gospels who weave their stories around the life of Jesus did so because they wanted to portray Jesus as having miraculous powers and draw the reader towards that conclusion, which would then require a response to

Jesus. They would also attach details to the stories about Jesus to emphasise the message they were trying to convey, such as when they describe Jesus as conversing with a prostitute, or when they place Pharisees (religious rulers of the day) together with "sinners", both of which would never have occurred. Bultmann argues that these little stories, created for emphasis of the message of Christ, are not essential for the message; there is a need for these accounts to be demythologised in order to return to the message of Christ.

WILKINSON and **CAMPBELL** note that "perhaps Bultmann's approach is mistaken. Rather than stripping out the myths from Scripture, perhaps the task of the believer might not be to deny that the myths are myth, but rather to accept that they are myths and to try to discern what truths they might contain."

Strengths

1. **TRUE MEANING** - The use of myth utilises story and a more flowing, lively and memorable narrative when trying to convey truths that might not fit other mediums. This might broaden our understanding of truths which could not be outlined in a factual manner but which nonetheless carry meaning.

2. **STORY** - There is a recent move to retell history such as the events of the Tudor Court, as story, and, in these stories, factual truth is used where it suits the story, but the fabrication of other details adds to the overall message the historian is trying to get across. However, it could be argued that the use of the word myth is inappropriate here, as there is still enough factual history in the retelling of the Tudor period for example, unlike the creation myths, which for many readers contain very little, or even no, factual truth at all.

3. **MORAL IMPETUS** Religious language, **BRAITHWAITE** argues, is meant to assert moral claims which express the desire to act in a certain way. In this way, they carry meaning in a wider way than can be measured by the **VERIFICATION OR FALSIFICATION THEORIES**. Braithwaite claims that the stories in which the truth is outlined give **MORAL IMPETUS** for how people should live towards one another, and do not need to be true for the "religious person to … resolve to live a certain way of life" (**JORDAN** et al) after listening to the truths contained within them.

Weaknesses

- **CHALLENGE OF SCIENCE** - The stories may have fitted a world in which the beginning of the universe was mystery, but now we have the theory of the Big Bang, it is questionable if the use of myth is still needed to convey truths or, in the words of **WILKINSON** and **CAMPBELL**, "fill gaps" which now no longer need filling.

- **CULTURALLY DETERMINED** - "Mythological imagery has a tendency to be culturally determined." (**AHLUWALIA**) Many religious believers want to say that there are central truths, or even a central Truth, that their sacred text is conveying, and these core elements might get missed or misinterpreted if myth is the medium in which those truths are told. "If a myth is just a made-up story like a fable, then it does not communicate any truths about God."(**TAYLOR**)

- **COMPETING MYTHS** - "There is no agreed criteria for judging which myth communicates truth." (**TAYLOR**) Napoleon once noted that history is the lies of the winner; how do we know that the myths that have survived are not those from the dominant worldview? Do such stories still contain truths or are they more like propaganda? Myths may change over time to respond to current concerns so that it is difficult to assess if they contain eternal truths. Taylor notes that an example of this is how in recent years Christians have interpreted the "dominion over nature" idea portrayed in the creation myth as containing the instruction to "steward" (caretake) creation, which has a very different connotation than that of dominion.

- **FLEW** - Might argue that it is convenient how stories in the Bible that were once held to be factually true, such as the creation story or that of Noah's ark, are now viewed as mythological, and carrying "deeper-than-literal" truth. If this is the case, have Christians who take this line shifted the goalposts as it were, and maintained the truth of holy scripture but by a disingenuous re-reading of text; is this "death by a thousand qualifications"? Christians might reply that this is now a significantly better way of reading the text, which is more true to the writer's intentions. But in doing so have they reduced sacred text to a series of nice pieces of advice, rather than the giving of Truth (with a capital, realist T?). Yet many Christians do not read the creation story or that of Noah and other stories, as myth, but as literally true.

Key quotes

1. *"The more real things get, the more like myths they become."* Fassbinder

2. *"The miracle stories added later should be regarded as statements of faith, stories told in the early Church. This is not a problem for Bultmann as the literal truth of these accounts is unimportant to the teaching (or kerygma) of Jesus."* Eyre et al

3. *"Myths are stories that express meaning, morality or motivation. Whether they are true or not is irrelevant."* Shermer

4. *"Through myth, believers are able to communicate something positive about God, without having to resort to the via negativa."* Ahluwalia

5. *"Because philosophy arises from awe, a philosopher is bound in his way to be a lover of myths and poetic fables. Poets and philosophers are alike in being big with wonder."* Aquinas

6. *"Myths and creeds are heroic struggles to comprehend the truth in the world."* Adams

7. *"It is a sure sign that a culture has reached a dead end when it is no longer intrigued by its myths."* Marcus

8. *"Old myths, old gods, old heroes have never died. They are only sleeping at the bottom of our mind, waiting for our call. We have need for them. They represent the wisdom of our race."* Kunitz

Confusions to avoid

A clear definition of myth needs to be used when writing about this use of religious language. Myth as "old wives' tales" is not the way in which the term is understood in theology and by religious believers.

There is a need for understanding of how different parts of sacred text are interpreted in different ways, so that when a believer says that the creation story is myth, this does not mean that a) it is less important than other parts of scripture or that b) the rest of the text is myth. Many Christians argue that there are different genres in scripture, such as myth, history, poetry, prophecy etc, and the reading of each in a particular way is respectful of literary interpretation.

THE USE OF SYMBOL

20th C. philosopher **PAUL TILLICH** wrote extensively about the use of **SYMBOL** in religious language, and how such could carry meaning.

Tillich argued that God is the **GROUND OF ALL BEING**, or **BEING ITSELF**. A crude illustration might help explain what Tillich meant by this: If you imagine a number of things on a shopping list, such as carrots, milk and tea bags, God is not one more thing on the list like any other object, which could or could not exist (many theologians have criticised **DAWKINS** for his description of God as one more thing on the list of contingent things). God is the list itself - God is the ground of all other things, being itself. For Tillich, God is the **ULTIMATE CONCERN**. If this is so, how is it possible to speak of, or journey towards, such Being (not "a being")?

For Tillich, **SYMBOLS** help us in this journey as they point **BEYOND**

THEMSELVES and, "open up new levels of reality". Just as a flag of a country can no longer be viewed by the winning athlete who sees it raised at the Olympics as a piece of coloured cloth, but rather as something that seems to take them on a journey of pride in themselves, their country and all that the flag means and represents, so a symbol such as bread and wine takes a person beyond the elements of bread and wine to ultimate reality, to being itself.

An example of a symbol is water, which is used in many religions. When water is used in a religious ritual, it is a symbol that enables those who are immersed in it to have the experience of purity or spiritual cleansing, perhaps even a sense of a fresh beginning. Now the water does not and cannot actually provide those things, but rather symbolises or points towards Being itself, which can be accessed through this participatory symbol. The way in which religious language is understood, and being used here, is both **EVOCATIVE** and **POETIC**, but Tillich is clearly claiming that it also carries some **COGNITIVE, IF NOT LITERAL, MEANING**.

Tillich used examples such as music and painting to help us understand how symbols move us towards a deeper reality, releasing in the observer something which only that symbol could do. However, to really understand Tillich it is necessary to realise that **STATEMENTS** about God, such as God is love, are symbolic too; it is not just physical objects that act as symbols but language has to be symbolic when talking of God as he is Being Itself (not just another being).

EYRE et al explain this idea when they write that whilst "we are familiar with religious symbols such as the cross or the bread and wine ... what Tillich is suggesting is that even statements such as 'God is good' are symbolic rather than literal ... Tillich refers to God as 'the ground of being', and suggests that this is the only non-symbolic statement that can be made about God". Here Tillich is meaning that statements about God are symbolic and participate in the reality of God, without meaning that language has ever captured what God is in a literal way. (Incidentally, this is an indication of the difference between a symbol and a sign, the latter only imparting one message to the reader, such as "no entry", or a 60mph speed limit, and not pointing towards, or participating in, anything beyond itself.)

To summarise Tillich and religious language - a symbol:

1. **ELICITS A RESPONSE**
2. **EVOKES PARTICIPATION** in the intended meaning (be careful here - look at the third quotation below)
3. **POINTS TO SOMETHING** beyond itself
4. **MAY BE UNDERSTOOD** on a number of levels

Strengths

1. **UNIVERSAL** - We widely use symbols in art, poetry or music to point us to something which is difficult to express, and this "beyond" to which it points does carry meaning for us.
2. **AVOIDS ANTHROPOMORPHISM** - The symbols of God's power and other attributes are not interpreted in ways which "describe" God or bring Him down to a human level; the opposite happens as symbols point towards Being itself rather than a being who is like a person.
3. **METAPHORIC** - It could be argued that we do use language in a symbolic or metaphoric way all the time. When we say that we could murder a cup of tea, we are not meaning that literally, but symbolically pointing towards the fact of our thirst. **AHLUWALIA** points out that when we say God hears our prayers, we do not mean that he literally does, as he has no ears, but the statement symbolises a characteristic of God (concern).

Weaknesses

1. **NON-COGNITIVE** - Symbols enable us to delve deeper into human experience rather than act as something that point us to any ultimate reality in which they participate. **EYRE** et al note that this is how **RANDALL** interprets symbol. The symbol does not carry any cognitive meaning, but is entirely non-cognitive. A flag might not actually represent anything other than citizens' ideas about the country, rather than anything "in reality". Postmodernists might argue that any reality is carried in the words themselves and not anything that lies behind them.

2. **AMBIGUOUS** - Hick has questioned what Tillich means when he argues that a symbol "participates" in the thing towards which it points. When Tillich talks about participation, he means that the symbol "somehow represents the event and gives access to a deeper level of understanding of the event" (**TAYLOR**), citing Tillich's example of music that takes us to reality beyond the actual notes to communicate feelings and emotions and even evoke beliefs. How does the physical symbol participate in the metaphysical reality towards which Tillich argues it points?

3. **MEANINGLESS** - What meaning does religious language have if it is symbolic and not literal? Is it actually saying anything of meaning? And even if such might carry meaning, who is to know if that meaning is correct, as what the symbol points towards is not available to us through experience?

Key quotes

1. *"Symbolic language alone is able to express the ultimate because it transcends the capacity of any finite reality to express it directly." Tillich*

2. *"When the Bible speaks of the kingdom of God, the symbol of a kingdom is concerned with the ultimate reality of God's power and rule." Jordan et al*

3. *"Symbols are meaningful on account of their relationship to the ultimate. There is an idolatrous tendency to confuse the symbol (eg a holy person, book, doctrine, or ritual) with the ultimate." Tillich*

4. *"Religion is the state of being grasped by an ultimate concern, a concern which qualifies all other concerns as preliminary and which itself contains the answer to the question of the meaning of our life." Tillich*

Confusions to avoid

Signs do not participate in the reality of that to which they point, and can be replaced "for reasons of convention or expediency". Symbols do participate and also "cannot be replaced except after an historic catastrophe that changes the reality of the nation which it symbolises". (Tillich)

THE VERIFICATION PRINCIPLE (VP)

Having studied ways in which it is proposed that religious language carries meaning, the **VP** puts forward a test to see if in fact that is the case.

From 1907 onwards a group of philosophers who had a scientific background attempted to define how meaning is carried in language and, according to **PHELAN**, "to eliminate metaphysics from philosophy". This group, known as the **VIENNA CIRCLE**, was influenced by **WITTGENSTEIN'S** proposal that the meaning of a proposition being put forward lay in knowing what is pictured by those words. The circle also built on the work of **HUME**, who had argued that statements only contain meaning if they are **ANALYTIC, A PRIORI AND NECESSARY** or **SYNTHETIC, A POSTERIORI AND CONTINGENT**. This distinction became known as **HUME'S FORK**. The Vienna Circle saw themselves as guardians of language in judging what statements carried meaning; the metaphysical did not, as it did not meet the criteria outlined by either Wittgenstein or Hume.

AJ AYER, who, I am sure, impressed his first wife by visiting the Vienna Circle whilst on honeymoon in 1932, approved of the rigorous test that the VP put towards language, and he felt that it helped philosophy to have clear guidelines concerning what language carries meaning and what doesn't. Building on the work of the Vienna Circle, Ayer published Language, Logic and Truth at the age of 25, and this became enormously popular as a classical definition of the Circle's **LOGICAL POSITIVISM**, whereby meaning is established in language.

Within this work, Ayer stated that a statement only carried meaning if it was: a **TAUTOLOGY** - true by definition (bachelors are unmarried men, which is an a priori statement), or **VERIFIABLE IN PRINCIPLE** by evidence (there is life on at least one other planet - there might not be, but, in principle with the development of technology, we could one day find out, ie verify it using our senses; this is an a posteriori statement).

Ayer's addition of the words **IN PRINCIPLE** to the verification criteria is often seen as progression from the very strict definition of meaning that was arrived at by the VP. The verification demanded by the Vienna Circle required direct observation of an event for it to have any meaning, which automatically ruled out any historical events. Ayer's **VERIFICATION IN PRINCIPLE** meant that historical and future events could in principle be verified. Ayer used an illustration from **SCHLICK**, a member of the Vienna Circle, to make this point when he suggested that one day we may be able to verify if "there are mountains on the far side of the moon". As such a statement was verifiable in principle it carried meaning.

In his first edition of Language, Logic and Truth, Ayer also wrote of a type of verification called **WEAK VERIFICATION**, in which he argued that there are general laws which cover many individual cases. To check that "a body tends to expand when heated" is impossible on a case-by-case basis, ie, impossible to verify; however, this is most probably the case, and the principle of weak verification accepts that there is meaning in such statements. This was different to **STRONG VERIFICATION**, which was when a statement was conclusively verified by sense-experience and observation.

Later, following much criticism of these criteria, Ayer would reject the strong and weak verification distinction, suggesting that the latter allowed for too many statements to carry meaning, whilst strong verification was too difficult a demand for most statements. He went on to develop a different distinction by arguing for **DIRECTLY AND INDIRECTLY VERIFIABLE OBSERVATION STATEMENTS**. Direct verification was possible where a person could check that, for example, "the tide is out at Weston-Super-Mare", or that "exit signs are green" - these are verifiable by observation. Indirect observations are statements about things which cannot be directly observed. **TAYLOR**, in interpreting Ayer's criteria, describes these statements as those that "could be verified if other directly verifiable evidence could support it". This would be the case, for example, with the observation of quarks, where all the evidence of other observable things points to their existence, even though quarks themselves are not directly observable.

Ayer makes clear that any religious or metaphysical statements fail the test as they a) are not tautological in nature or b) ever verifiable, observable, or supported by other direct observation statements. Thus, for Ayer, **METAPHYSICAL** language is **MEANINGLESS**. While disciplines such as history and science put forward either tautologies or propositions that are verifiable, metaphysical language (which includes religious language claims for God) does not meet such a standard. They are "factual non-sense", as there is actually no way of verifying such claims.

Ayer is not saying that religious language is false - it is neither true or false, as for something to be verified as true or false it has to have meaning, and such meaning comes through empirical verification of some sort. The statement "all giraffes have six legs" is false, but it is meaningful as it can be verified as true or false by observation. God exists (or God does not exist) is never verifiable; there are no means by which we can verify statements about God as true or false and hence they carry no factual meaning or significance.

Strengths

1. **RIGOROUS** - The attempt to define what is meaningful and meaningless could be seen as useful in helping to filter out statements that seem to be philosophically valid but in fact do not actually say anything. As **COLE** notes, Ayer felt that "through the misuse of language people assumed that because a word existed there must be some corresponding reality". Ayer has provided a useful check to counter absurd claims.

2. **REVISED** - Ayer's revision of the verification principle so that a statement can carry meaning if its claim can be verified in principle can be seen as both a strength and a weakness. It shows a philosopher who is willing to revise his theory, but this change might critically weaken what the verification principle is trying to achieve.

Weaknesses

1. **FAILS ITS OWN TEST** - The verification principle does not carry any meaning according to its own criteria. The VP itself is not analytical, and nor could any empirical evidence be provided to verify it. By its own standards therefore, the VP is itself meaningless. So how can its own claims can be true?

2. **VERIFICATION IS POSSIBLE** - The VP's rejection of any meaning in religious and metaphysical language is countered by **HICK** who suggests it might be possible to verify the claims of religion at the end of our lives. He uses the parable in which two people journey along a road, one believing that it leads to a celestial city and the other that it is leading nowhere. One of

these two will be correct, but the verification of which view is correct is not possible until after death. This is known as **ESCHATALOGICAL VERIFICATION** and meets the "verifiable in principle" condition.

3. **EVIDENCE** - It is difficult to know what sort of evidence counts when trying to meet the weak verification principle. What evidence is admissible? What if many people claim to have had a religious experience - does this provide empirical evidence? Can God be ruled out as the cause? With regard to the clause "verifiable in principle" **WARD** has noted that the existence of God is verifiable in principle by God himself.

4. **ASSUMES** - That the scientific method is the only way of assessing meaning in language. This is not argued for, and thus is an assertion which there is no obligation to accept.

Key quotes

1. *"No statement which refers to a 'reality' transcending the limits of all possible sense-experience can possibly have any literal significance."*
   Ayer

2. *"A sentence is factually significant ... if, and only if [a person] knows ... what observations would lead him, under certain conditions, to accept the proposition as being true, or reject it as being false."*
   Ayer

3. *"A proposition is ... verifiable in the strong sense of the term if, and only if, its truth could be conclusively established ... But it is verifiable in the weak sense if it is possible for experience to render it probable."*
   Ayer

4.   *"We ... define a metaphysical sentence as a sentence which purports to express a genuine proposition, but does, in fact, express neither a tautology nor an empirical hypothesis. And as tautologies and empirical hypotheses form the entire class of significant propositions, we are justified in concluding that all metaphysical assertions are nonsensical."* Ayer

5.   *"If we take in our hand any volume; of divinity or school metaphysics, for instance, let us ask, Does it contain any abstract reasoning containing quantity or number? No. Does it contain any experimental reasoning, concerning matter of fact or existence? No. Commit it to the flames: for it can contain nothing but sophistry and illusion."* Hume

6.   *"The Verification Principle eventually died the death of a thousand cuts."* Phelan

Confusions to avoid

Ayer is not saying that the statement "God exists" is false. He is saying that any statements about God are statements that cannot be **VERIFIED** (even the agnostic who says "I don't know if God exists" is putting forward his lack of knowledge about God as a meaningful proposition, when such a question could never be meaningful for Ayer). The purpose of the Logical Positivists is to create a method of verification which decides if a statement carries meaning, not if that statement is true or false - that requires secondary research to go and see if the statement is true (eg giraffes have six legs). To make this assessment Ayer argues that the VP is the necessary tool. Statements about God "fail" the test proposed by the VP.

THE FALSIFICATION PRINCIPLE

POPPER rejected the findings of the Logical Positivists and argued that the VP was bad science. He proposed that science should not be looking for continual verifications of its propositions, but rather **FALSIFICATIONS**. He used the example of Freudian psychology to explain this; when Freud argues that difficulties in adult life stem from our traumatic experiences in childhood, this is easy to verify as it is so wide a proposition, and Freud does exactly this when he suggests that every person requires psychiatric counselling. However, what marks real science out from what Popper calls pseudo-science is that a proposition should be able to be falsified. The VP might suggest "there will be sunshine somewhere tomorrow" whereas the FP will suggest "there will be thunder over Birmingham at 2pm tomorrow" - the latter is better because it puts forward something specific that can be falsified; the former can hardly fail and is irrefutable, but this is bad science, not good.

FLEW built on the FP to criticise religious language as non-falsifiable, and because it is, statements such as "God exists" carry no meaning. Flew uses the parable provided by **WISDOM**, in which he describes two people who come across a clearing in the jungle, where there are both flowers and weeds. One person argues that it is tended by a gardener while the other argues that there is no such gardener. The latter suggests that they watch for the gardener's appearance and even sets up elaborate traps and bloodhounds who would smell the gardener if he came in the night. No gardener appears, but the person who believes a gardener comes is not convinced that this has shown there is not a gardener. He suggests that the gardener is invisible, intangible, soundless and even scentless. The unbelieving explorer asks his friend who believes in such a gardener how his gardener differs from there being no gardener at all.

If a believer claims that God is love and someone responds by saying that a loving God would not allow children to die of cancer, the believer might reply that this is because of "God's bigger plan for us", or something along those lines.

Flew argues therefore that there is little difference between their belief in God and the belief the traveller had about the invisible gardener, and thus no difference between what they are claiming about God and there being no God at all. Belief must **ASSERT** something, and if it asserts something it must **DENY** or **RULE OUT** something too. If it does not, and keeps making exceptions, then it "dies the death of a thousand qualifications". (**FLEW**) As **PHELAN** writes, Flew is asking for "details of a situation in which belief in God would be untenable; the situation need not be real but simply hypothetical". Without providing such, religious language is **UNFALSIFIABLE** and thus is not putting forward a genuine assertion which is of any significant factual importance.

HARE devised the parable about a man who is convinced that his university teachers are out to kill him, despite evidence against this, such as his teachers' kindness towards him. His entire life, behaviour and reading of events around him are shaped by this conviction, which Hare calls a **BLIK**. Hare argues that such bliks carry deep meaning and they are widespread in the human community, similar to some kind of psychological conditioning. No one is without some kind of unfalsifiable blik which makes deep sense to us and through which we interpret the world. Hare argues that religious language does not make factual claims but imparts knowledge nonetheless, through the way it influences people's view of the world.

Flew responded to Hare by saying that religious believers are claiming more than he thinks, and are not just saying that their blik is one of many. What believers are claiming is something about the cosmos, in a

REALIST sense; they claim to be making assertions, which is what Hare fails to realise. If they are making assertions, Flew argues that these must be open to falsification (which they aren't).

A further response to Hare was provided by both **EVANS** and **HICK**, who argued that Hare makes a mistake in writing about bliks being right or wrong or sane or insane; if there is no way of falsifying them, then there is no way of judging what is a right or wrong, sane or insane blik.

A further parable in response to Flew was provided by **MITCHELL**. A French resistance fighter in **WWII** meets a Stranger who says that he is on the side of the resistance, and who convinces the resistance fighter so much that he trusts him. However, the Stranger tells the resistance fighter that at times his behaviour will look at though he is on the side of the German Gestapo. Despite some evidence that would shake his trust, the fighter, who represents the religious believer, maintains his faith in the Stranger, who represents God. He was so impressed by his initial meeting with him that there is enough to maintain his belief, even when the evidence against such belief seems quite powerful.

Mitchell maintains that the person's belief in the personal character of the Stranger is sufficient to enable the believer to sustain faith; religious belief has a quality, depth and reason to it that a believer will not simply abandon when difficult times come, and he argues that Flew has not correctly understood how religious belief operates.

In summary:
- **FLEW** - Argues that statements about God are not genuine scientific assertions as they cannot be falsified.
- **HARE** - Argues that religious beliefs, like bliks, are unfalsifiable but carry meaning.
- **MITCHELL** - Argues that the believer is aware of problems that would count against his belief, but these do not provide sufficient reasons to discard faith.

Strengths

1. **TRUE TO SCIENCE** - Many have argued that **POPPER'S** criteria for marking science from pseudo-science was a much more useful and valid move than looking for continual verification of a proposition, which actually does not move scientific understanding on.

2. **EVALUATIVE** - Flew challenges the believer to evaluate what is being claimed in such statements such as "God is love" or "God has a plan"; are such factual claims?

Weaknesses

1. **AHLUWALIA** - Suggests that Flew's "confidence in empirical evidence as the final test of meaning is, in itself, unfalsifiable".

2. **PHELAN** - Writes that the evidence required by Flew's falsifying test would have to be a) unambiguous, b) identifiable by everyone and c) non-jargonistic, and it is not clear if religious language works like that, or whether such is possible. He notes that it would be possible to falsify the belief that there is a loving God if it could be proved that the world works ultimately against our welfare, but that is a difficult challenge.

Key quotes

1. *"Hare is echoing Wittgenstein's point that religious beliefs are used to evaluate reality, rather than something that one checks against reality." Phelan*

2. *"Metaphysical claims about the existence and nature of God are obviously not open to empirical verification or falsification since God is not an empirically observable object." Brummer*

3. *"To say that religious sentences are not reducible to scientific assertions is a wholly separate question from whether they are true or false." Wilkinson and Campbell*

4. *"By saying that God is invisible, soundless, incorporeal and so on, there is very little difference between our definition of God and our definition of nothingness; we argue God out of existence by 'a thousand qualifications'." Ahluwalia*

Confusions to avoid

1. Do not just list the many scholars who have contributed to the debate concerning the VP and the FP. The parables given by the different philosophers were illustrative of major criticisms and you must use them in this way; if you do not draw out the meaning and expand this, then retelling the parable itself will not gain you marks.

2. Flew is not talking about the meaningfulness of religious language; he is arguing that the FP is a test of whether something is making a scientific assertion or not. Religious language does not make a scientific assertion because it cannot be falsified, which genuine assertions can be. Religious language may have meaning in other ways.

3. Note that Hick's eschatological verification might meet the qualification of the weak verification principle, in that it is possible to suggest that the existence of God is verifiable in principle, post death. However it is impossible to falsify such a claim. Hick was actually pointing out the limitations of the falsification theory, that whilst some things can be verified, such as the eschatological celestial city, they cannot necessarily be falsified.

WITTGENSTEIN'S LANGUAGE GAMES

WITTGENSTEIN did not so much look at the meaning of language but at how language is used. Words, when used within their "game", do not simply describe an object, but have a **FUNCTION** or **USE**, like **TOOLS**, which is how Wittgenstein described and viewed words. There are many "language games", such as rugby or music, and Wittgenstein's own example is that of chess, where language such as "move pawn to E4" makes sense, carries meaning and performs a function within the rules of the chess language game. Within that language game, if someone gave an instruction to move the pawn three spaces to the left, then that would be "nonsense", literally of no sense, as the instruction does not follow the rules of that particular language game. Similarly, if someone said pick up the ball and run 10 metres, that language is not appropriate or used in the chess game.

If you are reading this in class, there will be many language games going on in the school, such as in the Physics classroom, or in PE. Even individual words such as "mass" will have different understandings within the different games in which they are used - if mass is being taught in Physics it will have a very different meaning when taught in an RE lesson about Roman Catholic practice. To understand the meaning of the language, you must look at the activity that it refers to within its game.

These language games are part of life; when we joke or give thanks, we participate in a game that has particular rules. Language games are the way in which we enter into understanding of the world. Wittgenstein developed this idea further when outlining how speaking is a **FORM OF LIFE** shared with others; **BURNS** and **LAW** describe a form of life as "the activity with which a language game is associated" so that "talk of the love of God must be understood not only in the context of other things that are said about God, but also by looking at what it means in practice".

Because these games are forms of life, language is never private as it takes place and has meaning and function within its game, and develops within that setting. Wittgenstein would therefore reject any ideas that we can use language in a private capacity, such as carried out by Descartes and his claim "I think therefore I am". It would appear that Descartes thinks such a claim is formed by the private use of language whereas language is always a public discourse for Wittgenstein, and it is from such use in its form of life that it gains its meaning.

In outlining this philosophy, Wittgenstein deliberately moved away from his earlier support of the Logical Positivist's definition of meaning in language. Later Wittgensteinian philosophy allows for religious language to have meaning within its game, although it is followers of Wittgenstein, such as **PHILLIPS**, rather than Wittgenstein himself, who have developed his theory with reference to religious language. The statement "God is love" is very meaningful within the group or game in which that sort of language is used, whilst not understood by those outside that particular game. Therefore, it is not possible to offer simple verification or falsification tests to religious language, or indeed, any other language; these sorts of tests may be more relevant to the physical world, as **TAYLOR** notes, but cannot assess meaning in language. Language carries significance and meaning within the game through its use.

Wittgenstein argued that philosophical problems arise when "language goes on holiday". For example, if we take the word "soul" and think that we are talking about some physical object, then we are applying the wrong rules to it, and the "physical" game rules do not apply in this instance.

Strengths

1. **TRUE TO LANGUAGE** - The VP and The FP have limited use in explaining how the metaphysical is deeply meaningful, which is what religious language purports to be.

2. **TRUE TO RELIGIOUS LIFE** - As **TAYLOR** notes, "for many religious believers, religion is not a philosophical enquiry into the nature of belief, but a shared community life, culture, identity and practices".

Weaknesses

1. **ANTI-REALISM** - Wittgenstein has removed any **REALIST** claims that religious believers would want to make, such as "Jesus died for the sins of everyone". Christians would want to assert this as **TRUE**, as such statements **CORRESPOND** to an actual truth; they are not just assertions that make sense within the community of believers in a way which **COHERES** with other language that is used within the game.

2. **DIALOGUE IMPOSSIBLE** between people on two sides of an argument: the believer and the atheist. Language does not make sense just within its own game, but has universal meaning.

3. **CIRCULAR** Wittgenstein's proposal is circular. Words take their meaning from the language game which they are in, and the game gets its meaning from the words from which it is constructed.

Key quotes

1. *"The limits of my language mean the limits of my world."* Wittgenstein

2. *"Don't ask for the meaning, ask for the use."* Wittgenstein

3. *"We cannot get 'outside' the games to ask the 'real' meaning of words. We can only play another game."* Wilkinson and Campbell

4. *"The philosopher's task is to describe the way we use language, not to ask questions about whether or not things exist."* Burns and Law

Confusions to avoid

1. The meaning of language is found through its use in its form of life rather than its description of any reality. The issue here is if this anti-realist understanding is an accurate representation of what believers are saying when they make such statements as "God is love".

2. Do not say that Wittgenstein thinks each language game describes reality, even a reality that makes sense within that game; instead, each language game is using words in a particular and internally coherent way. No language is either "true" or "false" for Wittgenstein.

GET MORE HELP

Get more help with Religious Language by using the links below:

http://i-pu.sh/V7F53J34

Experience and Religion

KEY TERMS

- **CORPORATE RELIGIOUS EXPERIENCE** - Religious experience that happens to a number of people at the same time.

- **INEFFABLE** - Something that cannot be described in normal language.

- **NOETIC** - Knowledge revealed during a religious experience which is not available through other means such as study.

- **NON-PROPOSITIONAL REVELATION** - God reveals himself through the experience of the believer, accepted by faith.

- **NUMINOUS EXPERIENCE** - Awareness or direct experience of the presence of something "wholly other".

- **PASSIVITY** - The recipient is not in control and is being acted upon rather than initiating the experience themselves.

- **PRINCIPLE OF CREDULITY** - Unless we have good reasons to think otherwise we should accept that how things seem to be is how they are.

- **PRINCIPLE OF TESTIMONY** - Unless we have good reasons to think otherwise we should accept other people's testimony, including their account of their experiences.

- **PROPOSITIONAL REVELATION** - God reveals facts or truths about himself either through natural revelation or through Holy Scripture.

- **TRANSIENT** - A brief and temporary experience as far as time is concerned.

RELIGIOUS EXPERIENCE

A **RELIGIOUS EXPERIENCE** is sometimes used as an **A POSTERIORI** argument for the existence of God and provides unique challenges to the philosopher of religion. Careful definition has to be in place, and rigorous **ANALYSIS** and **EVALUATION** have to be offered, using specific examples (eg visions and voices).

SWINBURNE classifies religious experiences into **PUBLIC** and **PRIVATE** categories, though **JACKSON** notes these are not always as clear-cut as this distinction suggests:

PUBLIC RELIGIOUS EXPERIENCES are:

a. Where people perceive the action of God through an ordinary event, for example, in the beauty of a sunset.

b. Those which are observable but unusual, such as Jesus walking on water or healing a leper, in which natural laws are violated.

PRIVATE RELIGIOUS EXPERIENCES:

a. Happen to a person who then describes them in ordinary language. For example, Moses' experience at the burning bush (Exodus 3) or an angel appearing to Joseph to announce the birth of Christ (Matthew 1:20).

b. Happen but cannot be explained to others, for example, mystical experiences such as those of Teresa of Ávila.

c. Involve someone becoming aware more generally of the presence of God, which is interpreted from a religious perspective.

Religious experiences can also be divided into **DIRECT** and **INDIRECT** experiences. Direct experiences refer to where a person feels that they directly encounter God or the Divine. This could be:

a. **SEEING A VISION** - Such as described by the young girl Bernadette at Lourdes.

b. **HEARING A VOICE** - Such as described by Samuel in the Old Testament. (1 Samuel 3:1-21)

c. **AN ENCOUNTER** - Or a distinct awareness of a presence. **OTTO** describes this as the **NUMINOUS** or "apprehension of the wholly other", suggesting that God is above knowledge and logic. Otto describes it as different to the mystical which seeks unity of all things; a numinous experience is mysterious, tremendum et fascinans - mysterious, awe-inspiring in an overwhelming and almost terrifying way, and fascinating. It draws us towards the divine.

DREAMS that are recorded in the Bible (for example, Jacob, Genesis 28: 10-22 or Peter, Acts 10:1-28) are times when a voice or vision is described as part of a direct experience. But what do we mean by "direct" and "encounter" when a person is asleep?

INDIRECT experiences are when a person is moved or inspired by nature or in prayer and/or worship to think of and reflect upon the Divine, which might lead to a response of submission, repentance, confession and/or thanksgiving. **KIRKWOOD** uses an analogy to describe the difference between direct and indirect religious experiences: Imagine a person arriving at their house to find a bear eating the porridge, (direct experience) as opposed to arriving after the event to find clues that a bear has been there, such as an empty bowl and droppings on the floor (indirect experience).

"Some people have suggested that indirect experiences are not necessarily different from ordinary experiences; they are made significant by the person who has the experience and for whom the experience has religious meaning." (**TAYLOR**) The acronym **PIE** raises an important point about whether a person's existing perspective affects what type of interpretation they give.

(**P**) A person's existing **PERSPECTIVE** affects their

(**I**) **INTERPRETATION OF THE EVENT**, which affects their

(**E**) understanding of the **EXPERIENCE**

Would you interpret a sunset as light from a massive ball of energy reflecting on water, (through natural laws governing light and reflection), or evidence of the beauty that God has placed within creation? Does this interpretation depend on your existing perspective on the question of God's existence? **JAMES** argued that some people are unlikely ever to have a religious experience because they would not be open to such an event being a possibility.

Sometimes a person's existing perspective is changed through a religious experience, particularly during a direct experience (in which case **PIE** would not be the model to apply). This was particularly the case in the story of **PAUL** when he was not looking for an encounter with Jesus, but was trying to stop people speaking about Christ being the Messiah. This is an example of a **CONVERSION EXPERIENCE**; a more recent example would be the conversion to Christianity of CS Lewis, author of The Lion, the Witch and the Wardrobe (and much more!).

A useful question to ask is if any change in the recipient of the experience is far more likely to happen during a direct as opposed to an indirect religious experience. The question of how much our existing perspective affects our experience, or whether such can be changed and overcome in a dramatic religious experience, is also worth pursuing in an essay, and it can open links to whether a religious experience is "simply" a psychological experience, (see James later) a "feeling" or a combination of these, and possibly more. Are all of the above experiences simply events which make people view the world in a different way when a person has reached a particular stage in life? They might be influenced by a specific occasion that then shapes their life and subsequent worldview and psychology. This does not mean necessarily that the event was a "religious" experience, but that the event was interpreted that way. **HICK** regards this as "experiencing as" - where two people will view the same event differently and such viewing will affect the way the event and the wider world is perceived.

Religious experiences may be both the strongest proof that God exists for a person who has had one, and the weakest argument for the onlooker, as it is difficult to assess the evidence second-hand. Keep in mind therefore the question of whether religious experiences are **VERIDICAL**, and, if so, how; can they be shown to be what the recipient believes them to be, that is, "experiences of God rather than delusions"? **(TAYLOR)**

The Varieties of Religious Experiences (William James)

James found that there were four distinguishing features of a mystical religious experience:

- **PASSIVE** - The person who has this type of religious experience is not in control of what is happening; it is not willed by the person but they feel that they are in the grip of a superior power during it.

- **INEFFABLE** - It is not possible to describe the experience in normal language (see Swinburne's private experiences, point b above).

- **NOETIC** - The person receives some significant and authoritative knowledge and illumination, **REVEALED** through intuition rather than to the intellect, that could not be gained without this experience.

- **TRANSIENT** - The actual experience is short, (though sometimes time seems to be suspended for the recipient having the experience) but the effects of it are long-lasting.

As well as identifying what he felt was going on during a mystical experience, (which is an existential judgement) **JAMES** studied what such religious experiences meant for the recipient (which is a value judgement), and concluded that:

1. Religious experiences have a significant impact upon a person's life in that they:

   a. have great **AUTHORITY** for the person

b. are understood by the recipient to be **VERY REAL** (James was impressed by the **CERTAINTY** of the experiences he studied) and

c. can bring about real and **LONG-LASTING CHANGE** in the person's life. In fact, James said that the feelings of reality from a religious experience are more convincing than "results established by logic ever are", and that the results of the experience demonstrate that something of great value has taken place.

2. The view of the world, and our place within it, alters following the event; for example peacefulness, hope and love of others come more easily. The religious aims, following a person's conversion, become the "habitual centre of his energy". Whether induced or spontaneous, these experiences ("states of consciousness" - **JORDAN** et al) have long-lasting effects.

3. Religious experiences are part of a person's psyche, yet James concludes that there might be a supernatural element also. Neither was he concerned that they could be a product of neurosis, as **FREUD** would argue, suggesting that it was not necessary to have a "whole mind" to have a religious experience, marked by great certainty about the event. "For James, saying that religious experiences are psychological phenomena is a statement that a religious experience is natural to a person, just like other psychological experiences such as self-awareness or thinking." (**TAYLOR**) James takes an **EMPIRICAL** approach to religious experience, suggesting that these events "point with reasonable probability to the continuity of our consciousness with a wider, spiritual environment". (**JAMES**)

However, this does lead to the problem of whether a religious experience is just "real for them" and of no worth when used as an argument for a God who is objective, really "out there" (rather than in the mind).

What James was very careful to conclude was that the religious experiences he studied **DID NOT ACT AS PROOF FOR GOD** but that the individual had encountered what they perceived to be the Divine, the effects of which were very real. Religious experience "cannot be cited as unequivocally supporting the infinitist belief ... but that we can experience union with something larger than ourselves and in that union find our greatest peace". (**JAMES**)

Strengths

1. **OBJECTIVE** - James is someone trained in the medical profession studying similar experiences and effects experienced by a range of people. James is not out to prove the existence of God from his studies but to take an objective approach to what he finds.

2. **NOETIC** - We expect to find noetic elements if an encounter with a divine being has taken place. Whilst this leaves the onlooker no wiser as to what happened, it may be the case that description of it in ordinary language is not possible.

3. **EXPERIENTIAL** - James does not suggest that religious experiences bypass the human psyche, but includes emotions and feelings as part of the evidence for a religious experience.

Weaknesses

1. **TOO BROAD** - James' conclusions about religious experiences are so broad that religious experience could include drug-induced hallucinations. The lack of regard for how doctrine and creeds work to move the believer away from too much emphasis on subjective experience could be seen as a weakness in James' understanding of religion.

2. **PRE-DETERMINED** - If religious experiences are real it begs the question why people in different religions experience very different revelations. The doctrine of the religion seems to determine the type of experience (for example, the Cross and **STIGMATA**).

3. **LACK OF AUTHORITY** - James's conclusion that mystical religious experiences could be psychological in origin has been criticised, as, if this is the case, notes **MACKIE**, they lack any real authority, and are no different to other psychological experiences. However, God may have put that desire for him into people's psyche and therefore religious experiences are a natural part of personhood.

4. **ASSUMES REALISM** - James concluded that an undoubtedly real event has to be caused by a reality. Thus, God as a real being, could be the cause of the real event, if that is what a person believes. Is this a strong or valid argument?

SWINBURNE, in his analysis of a number of arguments for God, put forward two principles when assessing religious experiences:

1. The **PRINCIPLE OF CREDULITY** states that "if it seems to a subject that X is present, then probably X is present; what one seems to perceive probably is so".

    It is entirely up to the person who is listening to the account of the religious experience to prove that the person who had the experience did not do so; the burden of proof does not lie with the person who is describing the account.

2. The **PRINCIPLE OF TESTIMONY** states that people usually tell the truth. Swinburne argues that in everyday life, our default position is to believe that people have told us what they have actually perceived to have happened. The burden rests on the person who does not believe that we have told the truth to prove that is the case.

Swinburne recognises situations which would challenge the principle of credulity.

1. A person could be drunk or hallucinating or an unreliable witness.

2. Similar perceptions have been proved to be false.

3. It can be shown that whoever/whatever the recipient was claiming to have experienced was not actually present during the experience.

4. It is possible to show that "whatever/whoever the recipient is claiming to have experienced was there, but was not involved in/ responsible for the experience". (**JORDAN** et al)

The principle of testimony suggests that we should accept the statement about what has happened during a religious experience unless further proof is provided (as above) which suggests that the person is not telling the truth.

The most significant challenge relates to points 3 and 4. James has already suggested that the impairments suggested in point 1 need not necessarily bar a person from having a religious experience; however, how one disproves or proves that it was God involved in the religious experience seems a very great challenge as we are not talking here about the experience we have when we encounter another human being.

MACKIE also suggests that it is perfectly conceivable that a normally reliable person could be either mistaken or give a false account, and thus Swinburne's principle of testimony does not hold. The balance of probability "suggests that the mistake is more likely than the supernatural explanation, however sincere they might be" (in **AHLUWALIA**). Do the normal rules about how we recount sensory experiences apply in the case of religious experiences? **RUSSELL** also suggests that there are cases which meet Swinburne's criteria in which people have said that they have encountered Satan rather than God.

CORPORATE RELIGIOUS EXPERIENCE

A corporate religious experience is when many people seem to undergo the same experience and demonstrate similar responses, for example "All of the disciples were filled with the Holy Spirit and began to speak in other languages, as the Spirit gave them ability", **ACTS 2**. The annual Hajj pilgrimage by Muslims is another example of corporate religious experience.

THE TORONTO BLESSING (20 January 1994). Following a message to the Toronto Airport Church from visiting preacher Randy Clark, people began to laugh, cry, fall to the floor, roar like lions, speak in tongues and claim healings. The blessing spread to Christian churches around the world.

WILKINSON and **CAMPBELL** note that it would still be necessary to evaluate each person's experience as some might be carried along with the atmosphere, whilst others might fake an experience. Social psychologists also point to group hysteria.

What does Toronto show of a God who is love, which is a central Christian belief? Would all the events described above be consistent with existing belief? Does God take away human reason, and is it reasonable to think that God would visit "a small group in Toronto while doing nothing for the starving of Somalia or the persecuted [Christians] in China"? Wilkinson and Campbell have strayed into the dangerous territory of trying to guess the mind of God here, but critical analysis of corporate religious experiences is essential. We could apply the tests that James and Swinburne suggest to these unusual events.

RESPONSES TO THE IDEA OF RELIGIOUS EXPERIENCES

1. **COLE** - How is it possible to say that we have had an encounter with God if we have no previous knowledge of what God is? How could we recognise and identify the "other" as God? To say that the experience is one in which we "just know" it is God is philosophically dubious because, as **COLE** notes, it is based on a conviction rather than reasons.

2. **STARBUCK** - Carried out a study of **CONVERSION**, and noted that most religious conversions happen in late teens/early twenties when people speak of finding a peace through beginning to follow God. However, he found that, at that same stage in life, many non-religious young people also went through a stage of psychological angst and unease before finding their own identity in early adult life, and this process did not involve a religious conversion event. However, **EYRE** et al write that, in response to Starbuck, "some theists recognise that there are psychological aspects of conversion experiences but argue that to reduce conversion to just a psychological phenomenon fails to address the question of the cause of the experience".

3. **FREUD** - Argued that religious experiences are reactions to a hostile world, in which we seek help from a father figure. Human identity is marked by repressed sexuality, deeply imbedded into us from childhood experiences, which leads to psychological unease and unrest. Religion and religious experiences, argues Freud, are ways in which we attempt to deal with our psychological needs, but are simply childlike desires for a good relationship with a father figure (God), and they actually avoid us coming to terms, and dealing properly with our needs. **MARX** suggested that religion acts like an opiate to dull the

pain people feel in daily life caused by lack of economic power. **JAMES** argued that such a dismissal of religious experiences arose from those who were already deeply hostile to religion. Furthermore, many who have been committed to the cause of their religion, strengthened by their religious experiences, have found religion to be far from an opiate but something that has led to them being persecuted and even martyred.

4. **FLEW** - Suggests that it is not possible to give any credence to statements such as "I saw the risen Christ", due to the fact that there is no test by which we can assess if such a statement is true or not; verification and falsification are both impossible and therefore the statement is meaningless.

5. **KANT** - Argued that it is simply not possible to experience things beyond the phenomenal realm as we do not have any senses that can access a noumenal realm. Such may exist, but "given that human senses are finite and limited, it is impossible for humans to experience an unlimited God". (**EYRE** et al)

Key quotes

1. *"Religious experience seems to the subject to be an experience of God or of some other supernatural being."* Richard Swinburne

2. *"In the natural sciences and industrial arts, it never occurs to anyone to try to refute opinions by showing up their author's neurotic constitution."* William James

3. *"From a scientific point of view, we can make no distinction between the man who eats little and sees heaven and the man who drinks much and sees snakes."* Bertrand Russell

4. *"To say that God spoke to him in a dream, is no more than to say that he dreamed God spoke to him."* Hobbes

5. *"Religion is the feelings, acts, and experiences of individual men in their solitude in relation to whatever they many consider the divine."* William James

6. *"God establishes himself in the interior of this soul in such a way it is wholly impossible for me to doubt that I have been in God, and God in me."* Teresa of Ávila

7. *"The fact that a belief has a good moral effect upon a man is no evidence whatsoever in its favour."* Bertrand Russell

8. *"How things seem to be is good grounds for a belief about how things are."* Richard Swinburne

Confusions to avoid

1. **WRONG CONCLUSION** - James did not state that religious experiences proved the existence of God. He did state that the experience was "real" (you can discuss what "real" means), and he did say more than the fact that religious experiences are passive, ineffable, noetic and transient. I have read many essays that outline **P.I.N.T.** as this was all that James said about religious experiences. His conclusions are far more wide-ranging.

2. **PSYCHOLOGICAL QUESTIONS** - This particular topic has many links with psychology, and things such as how accurate our memory of events are (see brilliant treatment of this in The Invisible Gorilla and other ways our intuitions deceive us), how we can access other minds and what it means to have a psychological experience. The challenge for the philosophy student is to see if religious experience stands up to **PHILOSOPHICAL** scrutiny. The examiner will not expect, or want you to produce a psychological critique of religious experiences.

3. **FALLACY** - Students can be prone to commit the "fallacy of the excluded middle" in this topic: a religious experience is either real or an illusion (ie false). There might be another sort of **MIDDLE** experience going on, so that it is not entirely illusory that "something" happened. How one argues this **EXCLUDED MIDDLE** presents difficulties, but that goes right to the core of this particular subject.

4. **TRUTH CONDITIONS** - A reasonable way in which to assess visions and voices and other types of religious experience, is to see if they:

   a. fit in with the general teaching of the religion and

   b. lead to an outcome that accords with the teaching of that religion.

   This widens out the analysis from that specific experience; however, whether it says anything about the "truth" of that particular experience might depend on what one thinks of the "truth" of the religion.

5. **EYRE ET AL** - They rightly point out that there is a difference in saying: "If there is a God there are likely to be experiences of him" (a claim **SWINBURNE** makes) and "there are religious experiences, therefore there is a God". The former statement is less controversial though not necessarily true. The latter commits the fallacy of affirming the consequent (the consequent is the second half of the statement, or the consequence if the first half of the statement is the case). It is like saying, "I have a wet house, therefore it is raining", whereas there could be many other reasons why I have a wet house, such as my neighbour watering his prize roses. There might be religious experiences, but one cannot conclude from these that there is a God.

REVELATION AND HOLY SCRIPTURE

Revelation can come in many ways - through nature and conscience - known as **GENERAL REVELATION**, and through personal encounter with the "wholly other", religious experience(s) and through **HOLY SCRIPTURE** - the latter examples being known as **SPECIAL REVELATION**.

Holy Scripture has authority within religious communities precisely because it is holy or "set apart", and is therefore "special revelation". There are groups within religions who take the actual commands of Holy Scripture in a literal sense, while others regard the Church or religious authorities as the bodies that can interpret the meaning of the text for today's world. Whilst accepting scripture as authoritative and of divine origin, the latter group argue that there is a need to interpret the commands and teachings in a way which maintains the intention of those laws and concurrently speaks relevantly to today's culture.

There are different ways of regarding revelation through scripture, two of which are **PROPOSITIONAL AND NON-PROPOSITIONAL REVELATION**. Scripture has authority in both these approaches, but in different ways. In fact, believers can sometimes hold that God reveals himself in both of these ways - propositionally through scripture, and non-propositionally through other and varied religious experiences and through nature itself.

PROPOSITIONAL REVELATION refers to how God reveals his nature to people through propositions or truths in His Word. God's Word is inerrant (without error) because it has been verbally inspired by God. These truths or propositions are statements of fact that reveal things about God. The Qur'an is regarded as propositional revelation, whilst elements within Christianity regard biblical revelation as taking the form of propositions. The believer accepts these revelations because they are from God and such truths are not accepted due to their logic or because humans can use **REASON** to work them out. This means that for some who accept propositional revelation, the biblical or Qur'anic stories are exactly like they say they are (ie the creation stories), even if scientific evidence suggests otherwise.

However, **TAYLOR** notes that, for many believers, the use of reason is not rejected, but that, for those that believe in propositional revelation, "God's revelations are not provable by reason". Indeed, the Roman Catholic position, whilst propositional, stresses the idea that God has revealed his laws through reason and this will align with the Word of God, which still needs to be interpreted to speak to Christians today. It is important to note that one can take a propositional approach to Scripture without interpreting the Bible literally in a word for word manner. **AQUINAS** argued that God can also be revealed in the world through **NATURAL THEOLOGY**, such as evidence of causation in the world that leads to the idea of a first cause. Again, these natural revelations will agree with the propositional revelation God makes of himself in scripture.

A person who accepts propositional revelation will regard scripture as the **WORD OF GOD** in which the authors are passive recipients of God's revelation to humanity. The authors were under the direction of God to record his revelation, and these revelations reveal God's nature and will. The Bible is regarded as "divinely spoken"/the Word of God. However, some who regard scripture as propositional revelation also believe that the authors have a role in recording the revelation in their own language and styles. Indeed, there are passages where the human voice is very strongly in evidence (see Psalm 51); many Christians view this as divinely inspired, but would not take out the human element from it. This is in contrast to a more fundamentalist position in which the authors are passive channels through which God delivers his word. Both these views regard scripture as without error in revealing God's will and nature.

NON-PROPOSITIONAL KNOWLEDGE is not factual in nature, but refers to a different sort or sorts of knowledge such as the skill to do something like driving a car or speaking in another language. Non-propositional revelation refers to the knowledge of God which is seen through what he has done in the world, or through his guidance, or through the example of Christ. Taylor notes, that, in this view, the believer recognises the actions of God in history and human experience. This evidence which leads to the belief that God has acted is both **INTERPRETATIVE** and **INDIRECT**.

With regard to Holy Scripture, non-propositional revelation refers to the way in which God is seen to have acted in history, as recorded by people through their experiences. Non-propositional revelation revolves around **FAITH IN** something rather than **FAITH THAT** something is the case. **BUBER** stressed the need to view faith as an I-Thou relationship, rather than in an I-It sense, where truth-seeking propositional-type questions about "what God is" are replaced by "who art Thou?", and the stress is on a relational rather than a factual approach.

Those who wrote about Christ or witnessed his work interpreted such events, through faith, as God's work, as does the believer when they read the record of it. If the Bible is regarded as non-propositional revelation, the role of the reader and how the reader interprets the Bible will be of crucial importance, because the non-propositional revelation takes place in the life of the believer. You should note here the differences between this and the propositional/Truth way of regarding Scripture, where the role of the author and reader of holy text is limited to a more passive reception of the revelation of the Word of God.

To stress, the author and the reader play a vital role in the non-propositional approach to revelation and faith becomes a way of seeing and interpreting the world. Christ is received by faith from the "inspired words of the Bible", rather than through acceptance of propositional truth statements from the Word of God, as the reader interprets the text and story.

The Bible is seen to point to Christ, the Word of God, rather than be the Word of God itself.

SCHLEIERMACHER was associated with this approach, which stressed the need for the experiential in the religious life. **TAYLOR** notes that in Schleiermacher's approach Christ was regarded as someone who raised awareness of God rather than one to be accepted propositionally as the one who saves people.

BARTH strongly rejected this view, arguing that God alone, not nature or reason, provides knowledge through revelation. When attempts are made to combine faith and reason to understand the revelation of God, as seen in the work of **AQUINAS**, Barth argued that people quickly go wrong. Barth's claim that divine revelation is not the same as human insight, notes **AHLUWALIA**, limits God's revelation to his action, not human interpretation.

Strengths

1. **UNCHANGING** - If God is unchanging and has revealed his will and nature, then propositional revelation gives an account of a set of teachings and laws which do not change according to the latest human fads. God is given due regard as one who is the eternal source of right revelation, not interpreted by fallible humanity; this also means right moral decisions can be made according to the guidance of propositional revelation.

2. **TRUE TO GOD** - The propositional account gives a high status to the Word of God as infallible, ie, without error, which one might expect if it is revelation from God.

3. **FLEXIBLE** - Non-propositional revelation gives due regard to the idea that the reader of the Bible can use their capacity to interpret and understand it in a way which retains their freedom. The reader is seen to be active in the receipt and interpretation of revelation which respects their dignity and enables them to see the Bible as part of life, deeply influential upon their worldview and adopted through their freely chosen faith response to it.

Weaknesses

1. **IMPLAUSIBLE** - Can we ever be truly passive in our psyche when receiving revelation? Is there always an interpretive element to it? Can we be sure that the revelation humanity is purported to have received through God's propositional disclosure is as God intended, and how do we know if the authors have remembered such revelation correctly when memory can play tricks?

2. **REJECTED** - Can we ever be sure what a true proposition is and what is not? What about the different truth claims that are made both within, and between, religions, for example, about the status of Jesus Christ as either the Son of God in Christianity or a prophet in Islam? How can propositional revelation stay relevant when some of the views revealed in scripture have been seen to be rejected by many modern-day societies?

3. **READER RELATIVE** - Non-propositional revelation puts too much emphasis on the interpretation of the event by the reader. There are no infallible "facts" over which one is in dispute; the reader interprets what the biblical text reveals, and in what way he interprets the world as a non-propositional revelation of God. There are many different ways of looking at the world if no facts are revealed and it is difficult to know why one worldview should be seen as more authoritative than another, which is very different to those who regard revelation as propositional. However, **WILKINSON** and **CAMPBELL** point out that there is a link between the two types of revelation because people don't just believe, non-propositionally, in something (Latin "fiducia") without paying regard to what ("fides") that something is propositionally - many people believe that the Word of God is to be accepted propositionally whilst "believing no less fervently in Jesus as personal Saviour".

Key quotes

1. *"Revealed theology concerns those truths about God which are only knowable through God's special revelation, such as the Trinity or the divine nature of Jesus. This distinction is generally rejected by those who hold a non-propositional view." Wilkinson and Campbell.*

2. *"Since the creation of the world, his invisible qualities, his eternal power and divine nature, have been clearly seen, being understood through what he has made." Paul on General Revelation. "All Scripture is God-breathed and is useful for teaching, rebuking, correcting and training in righteousness." 1 Timothy 3:16, on Special Revelation*

3. *Muslims believe that "when a person who is not necessarily a believer reads the Qur'an sincerely and without ulterior motives, they readily recognise that it is a holy book and are converted. The propositions in the Qur'an have such power because they are dictated by Gabriel to the Prophet." The Bible never makes this claim - it was written by many authors from stories spanning centuries*

4. *"The distinction between propositional and non-propositional approaches is theologically and philosophically valuable, but it is not the whole story of faith as lived." Wilkinson and Campbell*

Confusions to avoid

1. The propositionalist position is not a literalist position. The Roman Catholic approach accepts that the Bible is the Word of God whilst recognising the need to understand the time, culture and intentions of the authors.

2. Propositional revelation can be viewed as "belief that such a proposition is true, whereas non-proposition makes reference to belief in someone, as a statement of trust, involving a commitment rather than intellectual assent." (**WILKINSON** and **CAMPBELL**) Non-propositional revelation can be "conveyed ... through art, music, dance, metaphor and symbol". (**AHLUWALIA**)

3. Don't say of the Bible that because something is not "true" in a literal sense it can be dismissed as having no meaning, as different genres in the Bible, such as poetry and prophecy, are interpreted differently.

GET MORE HELP

Get more help with Experience and Religion by using the links below:

http://i-pu.sh/W1J29D94

Miracles

KEY TERMS

- **DEISM** - The belief that God has no further involvement in the world after creating it.

- **INDUCTION** - "Instances of which we have had no experience resemble those of which we have had experience." (Hume)

- **MIRACLE** - From the Latin "miraculum" - an object of wonder.

- **THEISM** - The belief that God not only creates the world but is actively involved in it through miracles.

Three key definitions of miracle will be explored. Each requires different analyses and evaluation.

DEFINITION 1: BREAKING NATURAL LAW

In An Enquiry Concerning Human Understanding, **HUME** defined a miracle as:

A transgression of a natural law by a particular volition of the deity.

It is important to realise here that Hume is not saying that a miracle is simply an extraordinary or unusual event, but one which breaks natural law, and is carried out through the will of the deity. This was in contrast to **AQUINAS**, who, in one description of miracle, suggested that God could speed up nature, or do things in a different way to nature, neither of which required the breaking of a natural law.

An example of a transgression of a natural law in the Bible is seen in **JOSHUA 10**, where the sun is recorded as standing still in the sky for a full day. The natural law of the rotation of the Earth is broken during that event. Using his definition, Hume argued against viewing such events as miracles. As an empiricist, he argued that knowledge requires evidence, and we have to take a sceptical approach to anything requiring our assent. Bearing this in mind, his argument against miracles was as follows:

1. There is evidence for the idea that the laws of nature are highly likely to hold; these are established through many trials and repetition of experiments, as well as experience, and we make judgements about future likelihood of events based on these previous examples. We have countless examples of the sun rising and therefore it is highly probable that it will rise and not stand still in the sky. This projecting forward to suggest future events will take place based on previous evidence is called the **PRINCIPLE OF INDUCTION**. Hume did accept that what

happened countless times in the past did not guarantee such would happen again in the future, even though that would probably be the case. Because of this problem of induction, it is necessary to look both at the evidence and the testimony of witnesses to assess its likelihood.

2. Once we do this, then Hume says that we must ask the question, is there more evidence for a miracle occurring or for the natural law holding? Hume's empiricism was expressed thus: "a wise man proportions his belief according to the evidence". He adds that the evidence for the miracle would have to be so persuasive and strong as to overthrow the evidence that supports the existence of natural laws, which is considerable. As he notes, "no testimony is sufficient to establish a miracle unless the testimony be of such a kind, that its falsehood would be more miraculous, than the fact which it endeavours to establish". He went on to say that no such evidence for miracles exists which would allow us to suspend our understanding that natural laws are not broken, and that it would be "irrational to believe the highly improbable as this is to believe against the evidence." (**WILKINSON** and **CAMPBELL**) The balance of probability is against the miracle having taken place.

3. Now that such probability has been established by the appeal to empirical evidence, Hume looks at the event itself and those who witnessed it. When he looks at the quality of the witnesses to the supposed miracles, Hume notes that they are not of sufficient quality to give us reason to believe their reports - there is not "a sufficient number of men, of such unquestioned good sense, education and learning, as to secure us against all delusion in themselves".

4. Hume further argues that we are so prone to want to believe in the unusual, and that a miracle has happened, that this is sometimes the reason we believe such has actually happened; those within religion who know that a miracle did not happen continue to tell the story that it did in order to aid the spread of their faith.

5. Hume then argues that miracle stories take place in "ignorant and barbarous nations" which have not been enlightened by reason or follow the sceptic's requirement for empirical evidence.

6. The fact that different religions make truth claims and back up those claims with miracles, cancels all miracles out, argues Hume. As **JACKSON** explains: "the differing claims of the many religions result in them being mutually exclusive. Miracles are often presented as proof to the claims of religious belief, but if beliefs differ so much from one religion to another, then it only results in claims cancelling each other out."

Responses to Hume

1. Hume seems to be working with a model of natural laws in which those laws are more fixed and unalterable than is actually the case; this model would discount many advances in science where laws have been seen to be clarified or changed by exceptions to those laws. Laws are descriptive, not prescriptive, and likely to change as understanding increases. **SWINBURNE** argued that a law of nature "is the best description of how the world works that we currently have", (**TAYLOR**) but which could be modified through a new discovery. Natural laws are **PROBABILISTIC**, not deterministic.

2. What does Hume mean by "people of sufficient number and education" being required to witness a miracle? How many would need to testify to the event taking place? What level of education is required before they can be believed? What would Hume say to modern-day claims to miracles, such as those that have been studied carefully by medical practitioners at Lourdes? **VARDY** argues that Hume's criticisms only apply to the quality of the witnesses to a miracle. What would Hume think if a miracle happened to him?

3. In reference to Hume's wider work many have pointed out the logical **PROBLEM OF INDUCTION** - indeed, Hume was well aware of this himself. Induction is only true if the principle behind induction is true, or as **WILKINSON** and **CAMPBELL** write, "the only proof we have that many instances of events giving us probable general conclusions is the many instances of events giving us probable general conclusions". It is questionable then if this principle can be used to discount the occurrence of miracles; what if miracles are the exception to the inductive instances and that instead of induction predicting an exact future, it just predicts probabilities? Although most but not all testimony may support the uniformity of natural laws, miracles could still occasionally (by their nature they are occasional/unusual) take place. The least we can say is that the problem of induction leaves the door open to examples which go against previous instances of natural laws, however numerous observed repetitions of those laws there are.

4. Following on from the above, why would the improbability of the event mean that it did not or could never happen? There are many things which are most unlikely that take place where the balance of probability was stacked against that event occurring.

AHLUWALIA wonders if Hume is guilty of making a "jump from what is improbable to what is beyond rational acceptance". Believers might say that precisely because it is improbable it is more likely that God has intervened in nature. God may, as **POLKINGHORNE** notes, act in new and unexpected ways as a situation demands. Or, as **SWINBURNE** notes, because laws are probabilistic and not fixed, there could be events that take place that are unlikely, but don't actually break the laws of nature.

5. Why do miracles in different religions cancel each other out? **SWINBURNE** claims this would only be the case if they were incompatible with one another.

6. **SWINBURNE** (for whom the principle of credulity and the principle of testimony would also be relevant in the case of miracle), argues that we gain our knowledge of miracles from memory, the testimony of others and the physical traces left behind after an event (for example, the grave clothes of Christ in the tomb). These are the three types of evidence used for scientific laws; he concludes therefore that "if the evidence is not sufficient to establish the occurrence of a miracle then neither is it sufficient to establish the certainty of a natural law". Hume famously rejected accounts of miracles that had been experienced at the grave of Abbe Paris, a well-known Jesuit, despite these being witnessed by credible and reputable people. When Hume notes that we must reject these accounts because we have to oppose the "cloud of witnesses" with the "absolute impossibility or miraculous nature of the events to which they relate", is he judging the case before he looks at the **EMPIRICAL** evidence?

DEFINITION 2: CREATION ACTIVITY

In God's Action in the World, **WILES** moved away from Hume's idea, which expressed a traditional understanding of miracles as one-off events at the will of a deity. He attempted to broaden the understanding of miracle, arguing that this is compatible with the ideas of early Christians, who, notes **AHLUWALIA**, saw "creation itself and all the regularities of the working of nature [as] entirely dependent on the will of God". In Wiles' view, God's action in creating the world should be understood as much broader than one-off events where God has suddenly intervened in a situation. Rather, as he notes, "the idea of divine action should be in relation to the world as a whole".

The idea of God intervening occasionally and randomly in the world is not impossible scientifically or on rational grounds for Wiles; God could do this, but it would have to be infrequently otherwise the laws of nature would no longer be laws that held in the majority of cases. However, this traditional view of miracles is not defensible from a **MORAL** standpoint for Wiles, as there are just too many times when God doesn't intervene, such as in the horrors of the concentration camps. This lack of intervention on occasions and his action at some other, more trivial times, makes God very **ARBITRARY** and not worthy of worship. To heal someone's bad back and yet not stop terrible events such as an earthquake killing thousands is not morally or theologically defensible; however, viewing the creation and sustaining of the whole of the world as the single way in which God has acted gets over this difficulty raised by the traditional, and Humean, view of miracles, and in doing so helps Christians defend the concept of miracle in the face of evil. "Underlying all of [Wiles'] work is a very lively awareness of the presence of God behind the world, performing a single miracle of creation." (**WILKINSON** and **CAMPBELL**)

Furthermore, Wiles suggested that the interventionist-type miracles, such as the virgin birth, are not actually essential for the Christian faith in the way in which they have been portrayed, and that faithfulness to Christ without the need for dramatic signs or interventions was actually what Christ himself stressed. Wiles argues that the meaning, not the process, of the "miracle" is what is important, and the lack of historical verification for the actual miracles, as direct interventions of God, does not matter if they are **SYMBOLICALLY** understood. However, Christians who are **REALISTS** have faith in an actual virgin birth and an actual resurrection of Christ where God breaks natural laws and intervenes in history in the life of Christ.

Responses to Wiles

1. **SWINBURNE** responds to Wiles by saying that a loving parent would actually bend the rules in response to pleading by their children, but would not do this too often as it would take away responsibility the child bears for their actions. Wiles' idea of miracle changes the traditional understanding of God's nature, which is of a being who is loving, powerful and responsive to his creation.

2. What would be the purpose of praying if God will not intervene in specific situations? Wiles' view goes against much of Christian tradition and understanding; even though the reasons why God does not seem to intervene in some situations but does so in others does mystify Christians, they would not be willing to give up the belief that God does intervene. The biblical picture does seem to suggest a God who intervenes in human history, which would be the view held by **THEISTS**, as opposed to **DEISTS**, (see key words) which Wiles might be. However, **EYRE** et al note

that maybe Wiles changes the idea of prayer from being viewed as a long list of things which a person would like God to fix, to "allowing an individual to connect with God's will".

3. Has Wiles attempted to rationalise the actions of God in human terms? Whilst many Christians find it difficult to see why God doesn't seem to intervene in certain situations, this might be precisely because it is God who is acting and not a human being acting according to human reason. Wiles perhaps missed the point of miracles, which are to reveal something of the nature of God, rather than just to rescue people? "A comparatively small miracle might be more significant because of what it shows of God." **AHLUWALIA**.

DEFINITION 3: IMPROBABILITY

Miracles are extraordinary consequences, in which no laws of nature are broken, but where events happen together in a most unlikely manner. The person witnessing these events interprets them as miracles. **HOLLAND** tells the story of how a train stops just before it hits a boy who was on the track. His mother, looking on, horrified, interprets the train stopping as a miracle, whereas when the event was investigated, it was discovered that the driver had collapsed at the wheel and an automatic brake had been applied. The mother still thinks that a miracle has taken place. **HUME** rejects this because no law of nature has been broken, and there will be other times when the train does not stop and a child does, unfortunately, get hit. It is questionable if Holland's account is what people belonging to a religion understand as miracle.

Miracles are also **REVELATORY**. For a believer a miracle or miracle story might be interpreted as signs:

- **AUTHORITY** of God over nature.

- **FORETASTE** of the day God's will is fulfilled.

- **EVIDENCE** that Jesus is divine - a **CREATOR** and **REDEEMER**.

- **EVIDENCE** of God's continuing care for the world.

These signs depend on the interpretation of the person who witnesses or reads about them, and maybe miracles are meant to be understood by those who already have faith, not as something that is supposed to make someone have faith. Jesus' miracles have significance because they reveal something of the nature of God, which is why he refuses to do them "on demand" in the way that "magicians" of his day did unusual things to impress the crowds. The New Testament does not use the word "miracle" but **DUNAMIS**, meaning "power", or **SEMEION**, meaning a "sign of God", and this might be a better way of reading events such as the resurrection as signs of the power of God which reveal his nature.

In the Old Testament, **TAYLOR** remarks that people did not understand the world as one which was governed by natural laws, but one where the activity of God was seen through his "power and involvement with the world". In **JOSHUA 10** God stops the sun in the sky for 24 hours in order for the Israelites to win a battle and this fits with the power and involvement of God in the world as opposed to a suspension of natural law. As **TAYLOR** notes, "it is perhaps incorrect to see the miracles of the Bible as violating natural laws ... because the stories, particularly those in the Jewish Scriptures [Old Testament], come from a culture lacking any idea about laws of nature". God battles on behalf of his people to achieve his will and purposes for them, and the people gain this underlying meaning from the event.

MIRACLES AND THE PROBLEM OF EVIL

Here we ask a number of questions which can be linked particularly to **HUME**, **SWINBURNE** and **WILES**; the Bible is also portrayed as carrying meaning about evil, as outlined previously. You could also refer to the issues discussed in the attributes of God section later in the book:

1. Is God arbitrary and unfair? Traditional understandings of miracles (and the definition **HUME** uses) as interventions of God may raise the difficult idea that God is partisan, ie, someone who is not fair and biased towards certain situations. This is a moral and theological problem, as evil seems to be allowed in some circumstances where people have cried out for God to intervene. **WILES** recognises, and thinks he solves, this issue, but it is for you to evaluate if he has done at the cost of Orthodox Christian understanding of miracle.

2. Does the world have to be a place of hardship and suffering for us to grow, as **HICK** implies? If God did keep intervening through miracles, would that be like a parent who never actually allows their child to experience many of the potentially lovely and good things of life because those things can only be learnt through some painful experience, for example the process of learning to ride a bike? Remember **IRENAEUS' THEODICY** outlined this idea in the AS course.

3. If God always intervenes how could we have **PERSONAL RESPONSIBILITY** for our choices? And how would such an interventionist God show any respect for human freedom? Furthermore, the world's natural processes cause earthquakes and tsunamis - should God keep intervening in such processes when they are part of a delicate balance for how the world

works? For every day there is a tsunami there are many when there are not, for which God is not thanked; if people were being "fair" towards God perhaps blaming God for a tsunami should be balanced by thanks when one doesn't happen.

4. Should miracles be seen as **SYMBOLS** which carry deep meaning rather than literal events where natural laws are overcome? If they are, would this get round the problems that **WILES** raises and problems concerning evil and suffering?

5. How would we know if God had intervened to stop evil if that evil did not occur? Parents can often see obstacles ahead when a child is learning to walk which they remove. The child did not see the parent remove the obstacle.

Key quotes

1. *"A miracle is a violation of the laws of nature."* Hume

2. *"The gazing populace receive greedily, without examination, whatever soothes superstition, and promotes wonder."* Hume

3. *"Some people have suggested that stories such as Moses leading the Israelites across the Red Sea could be an example of God violating the laws of nature, but equally the sea and weather all combining to cause this great flood could be explained in natural terms."* Taylor

4. *Wilkinson and Campbell, in explaining Wiles, say that he is asking why God would make a party go better by turning water into wine, "where some had probably already had enough to drink, but do nothing to free the Jews from Roman rule? ... why make a statue drink, but do nothing for the hungry and persecuted in Darfur?" Wiles might ask why particular pilgrims to Lourdes get healed and not others*

5. *"The same event, described by the theist as 'a miracle', rationalised by the scientist as a 'probability of very low likelihood', may be reconciled by the philosopher as an impossible event that may have a divine cause if the divine exists."* Phelan

6. *"On the whole, Hume's scepticism is shown to be not so much destructive as pragmatic when applied to a real philosophical case study."* Phelan

7. *"It would seem strange that no miraculous intervention prevented Auschwitz or Hiroshima while the purposes apparently forwarded by some of the miracles acclaimed in traditional Christian faith seem trivial by comparison."* Wiles

Confusions to avoid

Work carefully with the definitions of the scholars. Read their views thoroughly, as scholars such as Hume, Swinburne and Wiles differ widely in what they understand to be a miracle, and critique of these views will be more successful if you have understood their positions clearly. If the understanding of different definitions is in place, it gives you more chance to analyse different examples of miracles clearly; it is better if you are able to work with some examples rather than talk about miracles in general. Hume, Wiles and Swinburne would have a different take on the same event, purely because of their different definitions which act as their starting positions.

GET MORE HELP

Get more help with Miracles by using the links below:

http://i-pu.sh/T1S35Z99

Life and Death: the Soul

KEY TERMS

- **AKHIRA** - Islamic belief in the afterlife.

- **ANATTA** - Buddhist belief that the idea of self is an illusion.

- **ATMAN** - Hindu name for the self, or soul.

- **DUALISM** - The belief that humans have a non-physical soul and a physical body.

- **MONISM** - The belief that humans are physical only. Sometimes known as materialism.

- **REINCARNATION** - The belief that the soul of a person is reincarnated into another person or life form post death.

- **RESURRECTION** - The belief that a person continues to exist after death in a separate realm.

- **SOUL** - The spiritual, non-physical "part" of a human, viewed as the centre of a person's identity.

Plato's dualism

Human identity and the question of whether anything of that identity continues after death has long intrigued philosophers. **PLATO** argued that humans have a **SOUL**, which is what enables a person to gain knowledge. Knowledge is gained when the soul remembers ideas from the **REALM OF THE FORMS**. The soul is simple, that is, without parts, and cannot be divided, although it is comprised of reason, spirit or will and desires; it should be led by **REASON**, as desires can lead it astray, and a healthy soul is when the three aspects work in harmony.

The soul, but not the body, is **ETERNAL**. It existed before it came to be imprisoned in a body, and will survive death, as it belongs to the realm of the forms. Plato's argument for dualism is based on two ideas: firstly, the soul recognises beauty and goodness as it remembers these from the realm of the forms - a person has not seen these in this world, but only shadows of them, and therefore the soul must have had existence in the realm where these concepts are; and, secondly, things get their existence in relation to each other - opposites such as light and dark are known in reference to the other. In a similar way, death and life are opposites to each other, so that "life comes from death, and death comes from life, in an endless chain of birth, death and rebirth". (**AHLUWALIA**)

Aristotle's monism

ARISTOTLE rejected Plato's argument that the form of something was separate to the object. Pure concepts like goodness and beauty cannot exist as properties separate to good or beautiful objects. Aristotle's idea of soul is that it is the very life-force of the human, our characteristics, or the **FORMAL CAUSE** of the human being. This is not separate to us, but makes us who we are, just as the form of an object is it characteristics; the axe has the form of chopping. This means that the soul cannot be separated from the body and that it cannot exist without the body it enlivens. This characteristic of the human soul is its ability to **REASON**, which is uniquely a human attribute.

It appears that Aristotle meant that the soul could not survive death as the soul ceased to exist when what it animated died; Aristotle has explained the soul in "natural" terms. However, Aristotle suggests elsewhere that reason could survive death as a type of "abstract property of intellect or reasoning" (**EYRE** et al), not as someone's identity.

Descartes' substance dualism

DESCARTES, as a **SUBSTANCE DUALIST**, argued that in the process of thinking, and even doubting, it was shown that the "I" existed. This "I" was the soul or mind, which is separate from the body. **RYLE** dismissed this idea as a "category mistake" arguing that to suggest there is a body and a soul is like proposing that a cricket team exists in addition to the batsmen, bowlers and fielders, when in fact the batsmen, bowlers and the fielders are the team in its entirety and it does not need this additional description of "the team". There is no mysterious "ghost in the machine", no soul in addition to the body, as if both could be spoken of as the same "type" of thing.

Taking a **HARD MATERIALIST** position, **DAWKINS** completely disagrees with Plato. He argues that:

- We are entirely physical beings, blindly programmed "survival machines", products of evolution and DNA mutation. Genes work to develop self-awareness, which is not due to a soul, but simply present because it has evolutionary advantages.

- To argue for a soul is an evasion which tries to explain consciousness without putting forward any evidence.

- Any reference to soul that Dawkins accepts is not the metaphysical, but the capacity for deep reflection and the feelings of which humans are capable.

- Nothing survives death, as there is no separate soul. Our consciousness is extinguished which was the case before we were born and so there is nothing for us to experience upon death. However, Dawkins suggest that **MEMES** are now replicators - that is, a person's contribution to culture and society continues post death, and has survival in that sense.

Hick's replica theory

HICK also rejects substance dualism. Unusually, he is a **MATERIALIST** who supports the idea of life after death, but does not favour the traditional dual substance of soul and body idea, rather suggesting that human beings are a "psycho-somatic unity". Hick argues that the soul is really a person's character or dispositions, and not something separate to them. Hick did suggest that there might be some evidence for an interaction between the brain and the mind in some forms of extra sensory perception, but this is not really similar to Plato's or Descartes' forms of dualism.

HICK'S REPLICA THEORY is a thought experiment which puts forward the idea that the resurrection of the whole person is possible. Because humans do not have this separate soul which would survive death, for Hick, any post-death existence would have to involve the whole person, which he thinks God could bring about.

- If John Smith disappeared in London and reappeared in New York we would presume it is the same person; there would be ways of proving that this "replica" would be identical to the original.

- Imagine if Smith died in London and reappeared in NY. Again, we could test if the Smith in NY had the same body as the Smith who died.

- The possibility exists that when Smith dies as a physical person in this physical world, an all-powerful God recreates him in another world of resurrected people. This person will have all the characteristics and memories and thus be the same person.

This can be questioned on several points:

- Is the body really a replica of the original if there has been a break in continuity between one existence and another?

- How many replicas are possible?

- Hick presumes the existence of God.

The **CHRISTIAN CONCEPT** of soul is of the **DIVINE SPARK** breathed into humans as the pinnacle of God's creation; humans are made in his image, and the soul is where God is experienced.

Strengths of dualism

1. **ACCOUNTS FOR MYSTERY** - We feel that there is a difference between a scientific description of the brain and that which we know as consciousness. Physical explanations of many events do not ever seem to get "inside" the event in a first-person way.

2. **PARANORMAL EVIDENCE** - Accounts of what appears to be the paranormal are well documented.

Weaknesses of dualism

1. **REGRESSION** - If the soul controls us, is there something else controlling it, and so on, and so on? This is the homunculus fallacy.

2. **BEGS THE QUESTION** - How can the non-physical soul or mind interact with the physical brain?

3. **NO NECESSARY LINK** - Plato's arguments can be challenged; there is no opposite for a rose, but a rose exists, and, why would something's opposite bring the other thing about, "or necessitate any kind of cycle"? (**AHLUWALIA**)

LIFE AFTER DEATH

CHRISTIAN BELIEFS about life after death, as reiterated in the historic creeds, centre on the **RESURRECTION OF JESUS**, who defeats the power of death, so that it is no longer the end for people. Mainstream Christian teaching is that his resurrection was **PHYSICAL**, which acts as an example or "first fruit" of what Christians believe happens post death. Paul writes that "when the body is buried, it is mortal; when raised, it will be immortal". **1 CORINTHIANS 15:35-44** acts an important outline for Christian belief. Although the resurrected body of Christ seemed to be different in character to a body limited by physicality, it is important for Christians that there will be a **RESURRECTION OF THE BODY** which will be transformed for post-death existence; however, this body is recognisable and identifiable with the person who died, which **GEACH** argues is the only meaningful way one can talk of life after death (in **TAYLOR**). Other Christians suggest that Christ's body after he was resurrected and before his ascension was a temporary body and not the type of body that he, and believers, will have in heaven, as this will be a purely **SPIRITUAL BODY** or just the continuation of the soul.

Christianity teaches that a person goes immediately to face judgement but some believe that the resurrection of all people and a final judgement takes place at the end of time. Other positions include the idea of the soul being judged immediately after death but then being clothed again with its body at the last resurrection. Yet others say this distinction is irrelevant as this all takes place outside of time. As well as different Christian beliefs about the exact nature of the resurrected body, Christians hold different beliefs about what the state of **HEAVEN** and **HELL** mean, with some Christians believing in Hell as a literal place of punishment and separation from God, and Heaven accessed only by those who have accepted Christ in this life. Others believe that God ensures everyone eventually gets to be with him in heaven, whilst some believe some souls (people) are annihilated after death rather than eternally punished.

CATHOLIC teaching stresses that souls go to **PURGATORY** where cleansing of the soul takes place to prepare them for the **BEATIFIC VISION**, ie, the meeting with God. After this cleansing the soul is united with the body.

In **ISLAM, AKHIRA**, or the afterlife, where body and soul go, is a place of separation between those Allah judges and rewards, who have passed the test of this life by doing good deeds, and those who have failed to show mercy and do good. Allah judges all people on the **DAY OF JUDGEMENT**. Paradise awaits those who have submitted to the will of Allah; some Muslims believe that punishment in Hell is eternal, whilst others believe that Allah will eventually show mercy to all.

CHRISTIANS, JEWS AND MUSLIMS believe in **RESURRECTION** after one life on Earth. **HINDUS, BUDDHISTS** and **SIKHS** believe in different forms of **REINCARNATION**:

- In Hinduism, the soul, or **ATMAN, TRANSMIGRATES** from body to body. The soul moves to its next incarnation after death, according to the **LAW OF KARMA**. The soul is clothed in **MAYA** (the unreal - flesh) whilst on Earth, but is seeking release so that it can be united with **BRAHMAN**, who is pure consciousness, ultimate reality. The birth-life-death cycle (samsara) is ended when the soul is released (moksha) back into Brahman after properly following one's duty (dharma).

- Buddhism speaks of **REBIRTH**. The idea of permanence, or "the self", is an illusion; **ANATTA** means "no self", a state into which a soul can be born and of which it is a part. Rebirth is seen as "not a continuation of the person's identity. Rather the consciousness of the person becomes one of the contributory causes in a new group of materials from which new persons are formed." (**EYRE** et al) Buddhist belief therefore is not about "souls" - the "I" is "not the person living his or her current life but the union of all lives lived". (**JORDAN** et al)

Responses to resurrection and reincarnation

1. If resurrection to heaven is only possible for those who have accepted Christ, or lived a good life, is this merciful? What implications does this view have for the idea of an all-loving God, as well as the problem of evil? In what sense does personal identity continue after resurrection - do people continue to age or grow? Paul addresses some of these questions in 1 Corinthians 15.

2. Is the person who is reincarnated "me" in any sense, and, if not, how can I learn lessons from a previous life?

3. Reincarnation might solve the problem of evil, as karma dictates that people get to face the consequences of their actions (any post-death existence attempts do this). But this might not explain why there is suffering in the first place.

4. **TAYLOR** suggests three arguments against the afterlife: it is wishful thinking, there is no evidence, and physicality cannot survive death.

THE NATURE OF THE AFTERLIFE

Is the concept of **DISEMBODIED EXISTENCE**, as found in Plato and in some religious beliefs, logically incoherent? This returns to the key issue of human identity.

If the soul is believed to be the core of a person, then perhaps that is where mental characteristics are located, but this would go against modern scientific understanding about the physical nature of thought and memory. Defences of the **LOGICAL CONSISTENCY** of the idea of disembodied existence include:

- **LOCKE'S** story of the Prince and the Cobbler, in which the two characters swap bodies and yet remember who they were before the swap. This questions if a person's real identity is in the mind or the body. Would this make disembodied existence coherent, as the real "you" can survive the death of your body?

- **PRICE'S** argument that the mind could exist post death in a mental world such as we experience in dreams, though this is criticised by **HICK**. Hick states that the world we all individually desire in our mental world would not be the same world as that desired by others, so there would be no shared world of mental perception.

- **EXTRA SENSORY PERCEPTION**, **TELEPATHY** or the claims made by **MEDIUMS**, where information is passed and received in ways that are "beyond normal perception". (**EYRE** et al)

- **NEAR DEATH EXPERIENCES**, such as that experienced by **PAM REYNOLDS** who was able to recount the words of the surgeons and the instruments used despite her having no sensory capabilities during the surgery.

LIFE AFTER DEATH AND THE PROBLEM OF EVIL

Some attempts have been made to defend the co-existence of evil and an all-loving God by looking to the afterlife.

AUGUSTINE argued that humans have brought about death and punishment through their own actions; it is gracious that God saves anyone from a (literal) hell which is deserved. Heaven and hell are part of God's retributive justice, which God has to uphold. Others disagree with this as eternal punishment does not seem a fitting punishment for small-scale (or any?) sin by an all-loving God. **SWINBURNE** argues that death and the afterlife make our free choices in this life have significance.

IRENAEUS argued that this world is precisely the world needed to move towards God, a journey which is completed after death. **HICK's VALE OF SOUL-MAKING** develops this idea so that the afterlife is the place where the **EPISTEMIC DISTANCE** between mankind and God is closed and everyone reaches fulfilment. **PHILLIPS** rejects the idea of a soul-making theodicy as it justifies evil, on a terrible scale, which is immoral.

KANT'S SUMMUM BONUM is not a theodicy; however, his postulates of God and the afterlife guarantee that there will be a state where virtue meets with happiness, as a rational universe demands.

Some argue that **REINCARNATION** does not solve the problem of evil: it does not explain the presence of evil in the first place, and if the self is non-existent, as is believed in some forms of Hinduism and in Buddhism, it is difficult to know how that self is rewarded or punished according to **KARMA**, which presumes personal responsibility for actions. It might also say to those suffering that it is their fault.

Key quotes

1. *"Football could not exist if there were no footballers, likewise redness could not exist as a property if there were no red objects." Eyre et al explain Russell's criticism of Plato's notion of forms as separate to objects*

2. *Replica is "the divine creation in another space of an exact psycho-physical 'replica' of the deceased person". Hick*

3. *"There is no spirit-driven life force, no throbbing, heaving, pullating, protoplasmic, mystic jelly." Dawkins*

4. *"To say that someone survived death is to contradict yourself." Flew*

5. *Buddhism teaches that "the new person is not identical to the old or completely different. They are simply aspects of the continuing stream of consciousness".*

6. *"Since we believe that Jesus died and rose again, even so, through Jesus, God will bring with him those who have died." 1 Thessalonians 4:14*

Confusions to avoid

Identify key themes such as "personal identity" and "continuity" and explore what those mean, with both clarity and correct reference to scholars and religious beliefs. Make sure you understand what "bodied" and "disembodied" existence mean when there is not this framework of Earth by which to make some sense of those terms. Critical reflection on the different understandings of resurrection, as well as differences between Hindu and Buddhist beliefs, could take you to a higher level of response. Be very precise with this topic as there are important differences in the positions taken, eg, resurrection as opposed to reincarnation, which raise different issues.

GET MORE HELP

Get more help with Life and Death by using the links below:

http://i-pu.sh/B5M37B57

The Attributes of God

KEY TERMS

Various interpretations of eternal, omniscient, omnipotent and omnibenevolent are precisely those that are studied, analysed and evaluated in this topic. Thus, it is not possible to put forward one definition of them.

- **ATEMPORAL** - Outside of time.

- **EVERLASTING** - God has no beginning or end, but moves through time with his creation.

- **IMMUTABLE** - Unchanging.

- **PROCESS THEOLOGY** - The belief that God changes and learns alongside his creation.

- **SEMPITERNAL** - Everlasting, inside of time.

GOD AS ETERNAL

In classical Christian theology, through the works of **AUGUSTINE**, **BOETHIUS**, **AQUINAS** and others, God has been held to be outside of time, or **ATEMPORAL**. An alternative view is that God is **EVERLASTING WITHIN TIME**, or **SEMPITERNAL**; he has **NO BEGINNING OR END** but **MOVES THROUGH TIME** as we do. These two views have implications for ideas concerning God's omniscience and power, and with regard to the problem of evil, punishment and reward.

If God is **ATEMPORAL** then God is unlimited by the human concepts of time and space and has full knowledge of the future. As such, he would be **IMMUTABLE**, in a similar way to concepts within **PLATO'S FORMS** and **ARISTOTLE'S UNMOVED MOVER**.

If God is **SEMPITERNAL**, then he is able to be described in terms of personhood as he responds to others, loves and is affected by relationship, which, many argue, a timeless God could not be. **SWINBURNE** argues that this is more biblically accurate, as opposed to the idea of a timeless God which he thinks Christianity erroneously picked up due to Greek influence. For example, God listens and seems to genuinely consider changing his decision when Abraham pleads with him not to destroy Sodom and Gomorrah.

This has some similarities to, but is not the same as, **PROCESS THEOLOGY**, put forward by **WHITEHEAD**, in which God learns alongside his creation; God, like us, is still "in the process of becoming" (**EYRE** et al). However, other biblical verses such as "God is not a man ... that he should change his mind", and "I the Lord do not change", seem to indicate that God's purposes are fixed and that he cannot change.

GOD AS OMNISCIENT

Understood at face value, **OMNISCIENT** means that **GOD KNOWS EVERYTHING**. However, such a concept changes if God is outside of time or if he exists as an everlasting being within time.

Influenced by Greek concepts of divinity, some Christian scholars believe that if God is **TIMELESS** and omniscient then all events are known by him as he sees past, present and future. This raises problems concerning human free will and responsibility, as events are going to happen which God sees and knows, and if God's omniscience is perfect, then that event has to happen and what appears to us as choice is not.

Concerning the interaction between human free will and God's omniscience, two types of freedom are put forward: The **LIBERTY OF SPONTANEITY** states that our freedom is limited because of our social setting and family background, etc. **BURNS** and **LAW** write that "on this view, the fact that God timelessly sees what I will do next Tuesday does not matter because my freedom is so limited; what I think of as a free choice could be accurately anticipated by someone - like God - who understands me completely". In this view, we can do what we want but even those wants have causes of which we may be unaware.

The **LIBERTY OF INDIFFERENCE**, supported by **BOETHIUS**, states that God having knowledge of all events in the "simultaneous present" does not cause that action. Knowing that a person is doing something does not in fact affect his freedom to do it. God sees actions as they take place, and this does not take away our free choice to do them; we have the ability to do otherwise.

If God is **EVERLASTING WITHIN TIME**, then he could be limited to knowing what we will do in the future in a predictive sense; knowing us as he does he could predict what we will do. If we have the liberty of indifference rather than the liberty of spontaneity, ie, real freedom, then that might mean God could not know the future as it has not yet happened. Some scholars disagree with this because of the implications it has for the idea of God's omniscience. However, **TAYLOR** notes that everlasting does not mean limitations with regard to the power of God; it means that "God exists without end at all points in time but not that God exists timelessly in the sense of Aquinas and Boethius".

SCHLEIERMACHER suggests that, just as in an intimate relationship one partner knows what the other will do without that knowledge restricting the other person's freedom, so God's knowledge of us is complete without it limiting our freedom. Scholars have questioned if this analogy works due to the difference in fallible human knowledge, even between close friends, and God's infallible knowledge. An alternative position is to argue that God has **MIDDLE KNOWLEDGE**, that is, knowledge of all possible futures which would arise if someone chose option B instead of A. But we can ask if middle knowledge exists, or if it is a "no-thing"? Interestingly, some scientists suggest that a new universe is created every time we make a choice; a universe in which we did not choose something is played out as well as a universe existing in which we did make that choice.

GOD AS OMNIPOTENT

If God is **OMNIPOTENT**, does that mean he can do anything, or just anything which is logically possible? **DESCARTES** believed the former, arguing that God would have limited powers otherwise. **AQUINAS** and **CS LEWIS** argued that expecting God to do the logically impossible is actually asking him to do a "no-thing"; ie, to ask him to make a ball completely red and completely blue at the same time is not a thing, but a nonsense, and nonsenses do not suddenly become sensible when expecting God to do them; literally there is nothing that God cannot do if logical absurdities are not counted as things.

BURNS and **LAW** note **OCKHAM'S** proposal which suggests that God could have made a world in which logical contradictions are not contradictions, though, as they point out, "this is not the same as saying that God is able to bring about things that are logically impossible in this world". It should be considered if logical paradoxes show limitations in our language rather than limitations in God's powers. There are also other things that God could not do which would be internally contradictory and against his nature, such as telling a lie or being unjust, or other things such as changing the past, but is this what is meant by God not having all powers, or just logical contradictions which, by their very nature, are not possible? Maybe, as **KENNY** notes in **TAYLOR**, "a being is omnipotent if it has every power which it is logically possible to possess".

There are several incidents in the Bible where God is seen to be omnipotent, such as at the creation of the world or, in the case of Jesus, the raising of Lazarus from the dead. **AHLUWALIA** notes that, in the story when Abraham is told that he is to become a father when his wife was a long way past child-bearing age, "God asks a rhetorical question 'Is anything too hard for the Lord?', implying that he can do anything and everything he wants to". Christian scholars such as **ANSELM** suggest that God must have all perfections otherwise he would not be the greatest possible being; he is not limited by the laws of logic.

Others scholars note that:

- this makes God capable of doing evil, which is a contradiction,

- to which the response is that we cannot grasp what omnipotence means from our limited perspective,

- to which the reply is that this is evasive as an answer.

Further problems with this view mean that if God can do everything possible and suspend the laws of logic due to his omnipotence, then he could have "allowed us free will without the consequent evil". (**AHLUWALIA**) The fact that he chooses not to do this is problematic.

VARDY'S response, noted by **AHLUWALIA**, is to suggest that God is self-limiting. He chooses to make precisely the world which works for the existence of rational and free human beings; however, this is a choice for God to work in this way, and "therefore it is still right to call God omnipotent because nothing limits his power except when he chooses". This is a self-imposed limitation, chosen because of God's love for humanity, states Vardy.

GOD AS OMNIBENEVOLENT

Important considerations in this section involve understandings of how good is used when applied to God. Is God "good" in that he is fit for purpose, like a good knife, or is God "good" in the moral sense, which has a totally different understanding? Euthyphro's Dilemma is directly concerned with the second option.

In the Old Testament one Hebrew word used to describe God's love is **HESED**, which can be interpreted as kindness, loyalty or concern for the welfare of his people, Israel. This hesed is undeserved and not given by God as a result of anything Israel has done. In the New Testament, Christians believe God shows this undeserved love to all people by giving Christ to die, and this type of unconditional love is known as **AGAPE**. The New Testament simply states that "God is love", which **EYRE** et al are right to note means more than "nice"! In the death of Jesus, Christians believe God combines love and justice.

This loving kindness is questioned by some scholars, who see the immense suffering the Jewish people have gone through in persecutions and attempts to destroy them completely. Furthermore, others argue that the love of God for all people is called into question when many people suffer through natural disasters on a massive scale. In response:

- Should analogy be used to describe the love of God, so it is understood differently to the way in which human love is understood? Or is **SWINBURNE** correct to say that God's loving reward and punishment are best understood through a parental model?

- Do theodicies adequately address and solve the puzzle of a God of love co-existing with the presence of evil and suffering?

- Is the response that this is "simply mystery" philosophically adequate?

- Is God, as **MOLTMANN** and other process theologians stress, suffering alongside humanity rather than outside of time, unchanged by it?

- Is life after death, where pains and injustices are corrected, a sign of the love of God? Should some people receive eternal punishment? Is it actually a good thing to have eternal consequences for freely chosen actions as it means our choices really count?

The problems raised above are exacerbated when omniscience, omnipotence and omnibenevolence are seen as co-existing in God's nature. Solutions to the **EPICUREAN TRIAD** (see AS guide) include denying one or more of God's attributes, modifying our understanding of what these attributes mean, or introducing another factor such as free will.

GOD AND REWARD AND PUNISHMENT

If God is omniscient in the sense of knowing all that is going to happen, and if his knowledge is perfect, that means those events will happen. Therefore, if I was always going to short-change a customer, or pay to sponsor a child, how can I be either blamed or rewarded for such pre-ordained actions? Responses to this include:

- We are not free as God has ordained what will happen; this is a **CALVINIST** position, in which God has eternally destined some people to be part of "the elect" and others for separation from him.

- **PROCESS THEOLOGY** suggests God learns alongside of his creation, and has knowledge of our actions as they take place. Any reward and punishment is the consequence of our free actions.

- God is outside of time; all events happen simultaneously when one is not time bound; all actions are known in the eternal present, but this does not mean they are not freely chosen by those within time.

- **SWINBURNE**, in advocating an everlasting God, argues that there is no future to be known by God as he is within time and the future has not yet taken place. We choose the future and God can reward or punish freely chosen acts, even if he might know what we will do due to his knowledge of us.

BOETHIUS ON KNOWLEDGE AND FREE WILL

In The Consolations of Philosophy, **BOETHIUS**, a 6th C. Christian, is comforted by Lady Philosophy who appears to him as he awaits death for treason. In his contemplations, he considers the problems raised by an omniscient God who knows the future. He considers how God could not have accurate knowledge if the future was uncertain, but also, if God did have full knowledge, how fair it would be for him to punish and reward, and if, in fact, God is responsible for man's evil actions.

Boethius comes to the following conclusions:

- God is able to see things differently to the way in which we do, as humans are time-bound, past-present-future creatures and he is not constrained like this.

- Because of this, a timeless God can view all events as simultaneously present.

- This means that God is not without the wisdom or knowledge about our moral choices "in advance", as there is no "in advance" for a timeless God.

- Thus, we have free choice and can be rewarded or punished, and God sees these events always in the timeless now. We possess the liberty of indifference.

With this background it is possible to understand how Boethius employs the concepts of **CONDITIONAL** and **SIMPLE NECESSITY**. God knows everything in the eternal now. However, some things, such as the sun shining, act according to their nature, and have to act in this way; this is simple necessity. Other acts happen because a person chooses to do them - there is nothing in a man's nature that says he has to walk, but when he is walking, he cannot not be walking at the same time, so he is necessarily walking, and God sees this event. This is conditional necessity.

Highlighting the difference between these two types of necessity, **WILKINSON** and **CAMPBELL** note that, if God sees anything in His eternal present, it follows that this thing exists necessarily in the way God sees it, "but it may not exist the way it does out of some necessity in its nature" (ie, the sun shining). And, thus the action being considered is key, and whether it is necessary because of its nature, in a simple sense, or necessary when chosen by a free agent, as a kind of condition - "if I want to walk (condition) then I will have to walk, and it is necessary that when I am walking I am walking" (necessity). Both types of acts are known by God, but when conditional, this is a freely chosen action. As a consequence, God has knowledge of the simultaneous present, ie is "timelessly-all-knowing", but our actions are freely chosen and Boethius concludes that God is just in rewarding and punishing such acts.

Rather than simply list strengths and weaknesses of these positions, it is better to consider **POSSIBLE OUTCOMES** of different positions:

1. If God is timeless, what sense can be made in the Bible where God seems to change his mind, or remember things or be surprised? Scholars who support the view that God is timeless suggest these verses should be read metaphorically, and argue that a time-bound God runs the danger of **ANTHROPOMORPHISM**.

2. To what extent can God be all-powerful if he is inside of time? All-power would contain all knowledge; such would entail a being who does not change, but an everlasting God would seem to change by his interactions with the world. If he does not change, it is questionable as to how real those interactions are, as every interaction humans have changes them.

3. In what sense is time a human construction? If it is, what impact might that have upon this topic?

Key quotes

1. *"To call God Almighty ... specifically does not mean that God has total power to do anything he wishes. God is limited by the universe he has chosen to create ... [a universe in which God wishes for humans to be] ' brought into a loving relationship with him." Note here that Vardy uses Almighty and not All-powerful - an important difference*

2. *"Swinburne does not see why a perfect being should have to be changeless; it was Plato who planted [that] idea in Western minds." Ahluwalia*

3. *"Before a word is on my tongue, you know it completely, O Lord." Psalm 139:4*

4. *"All the days ordained for me were written in your book before one of them came to be." Psalm 139:16*

5. *"I thought that you would return to me, but you did not." From the Bible*

6. *"It follows that divine foreknowledge does not change the nature or the properties of individual things: it simply sees those things as present which we would regard as future." Boethius*

Confusions to avoid

1. Be aware of the difference between the two types of freedom and necessity listed, as these are at the very core of the debate and can be fruitful ground in relation to the omniscience and, in some sense, the omnipotence of God. Read and evaluate Kenny's response to Boethius.

2. **WILKINSON** and **CAMPBELL** draw necessary attention to the idea that our understanding of eternal relies on concepts such as past, present and future; our language is tensed and we may face problems talking about a God who is not limited in the same way. Understanding the idea of eternity as an unchanging present is difficult when we conceive of God in a finite fashion, such as thinking, then acting, then looking towards consequences etc.

GET MORE HELP

Get more help with the Attributes of God by using the links below:

http://i-pu.sh/H2D97V50

Bibliography

- **AHLUWALIA, L** - Understanding Philosophy of Religion OCR, Folens, 2008

- **BOWIE, R** - AS/A2 Philosophy of Religion and Religious Ethics for OCR, Nelson Thornes, 2004

- **COLE, P** - Access to Philosophy: Philosophy of Religion, Hodder & Stoughton, 2005

- **DEWAR, G** - Oxford Revision Guides: AS & A Level Religious Studies: Philosophy and Ethics Through Diagrams, Oxford University Press, 2009

- **JACKSON, R** - The God of Philosophy, The Philosophers' Magazine, 2001

- **JORDAN, A, LOCKYER, N** & **TATE, E** - Philosophy of Religion for A Level OCR Edition, Nelson Thornes, 2004

- **PHELAN, JW** - Philosophy Themes and Thinkers, Cambridge University Press, 2005

- **POXON, B** - Religious Studies AS Philosophy, PushMe Press, 2012

- **EYRE, C, KNIGHT, R** & **ROWE, G** - OCR Religious Studies Philosophy and Ethics A2, Heinemann, 2009

- **TAYLOR, M** - OCR Philosophy of Religion for AS and A2, Routledge, 2009

- **WILKINSON, M & CAMPBELL, H** - Philosophy of Religion for A2 Level, Continuum, 2009

Lightning Source UK Ltd.
Milton Keynes UK
UKOW03f2238140214

226488UK00002B/2/P